THE PATH OF DARKNESS

The Path
of Darkness

RALPH HARPER

Cleveland
The Press of Case Western Reserve University
1968

The title of this book is taken from Verse 5 of the Easter processional, "Welcome happy morning," of Fortunatus, Number 87 of *The Hymnal of the Protestant Episcopal Church.*

PREFACE

For years I was impressed by the opening sentence of *Anna Karenina:* "All happy families are alike, but an unhappy family is unhappy after its own fashion." At first I thought Tolstoy was right, but I have since come to doubt it. It may well be the other way around. There are not that many happy families, and each seems to me to be happy after its own fashion. Unhappiness, on the other hand, is legion, and it is the unhappy who go through many similar experiences. I call these experiences of darkness, although I never forget the profoundly satisfying things that also take place in the dark.

I do not know whether darkness has a structure, or whether unhappiness can be systematized, and I am skeptical of the validity of all attempts to systematize interior experience. Nevertheless, I am acquainted with many kinds of darkness, and I know that some of these fall easily into several grand categories, and some do not. At the very least, I am curious about how they differ from each other and also how they resemble each other. I think we all should be.

One usually treats separately the somber world of tragedy (Chapter 3) and the contemplative world of the dark night (Chapter 5). The latter, however, is a special case of the larger question of the silence of God (Chapter 4), and the former a special encounter with fate, at the very bottom of the spectrum of melancholy (Chapter 2). I can go further and say that whether one is concerned about the causality of unhappiness or about meaning, the interior state feels the same and presents the same challenge to moral strength and the same invitation to wisdom.

Admittedly I proceed by indirection. I do not hope that what I say will be called definitive by some kind reader. I am, and I hope the writing itself is, too near all the experiences of darkness for me to pretend anything like that. And if there is anything new here it may be found not only in the range of discussion and illustration but in more subjective and more experimental aspects: in personal allusion, and in a style that combines fervor with analysis, irony with affirmation, lyric with dialectic. We are usually too ready to exaggerate the importance of a uniformity of style and thus limit our ability to remember and express the way things really feel when they happen.

Moreover, the range of experience considered here is unnaturally compressed. Few of us pass through so many clouds in such a short time. It takes a philosophically inclined man to observe the silence of God, and a religiously inclined man to feel the darkness of God. Not everyone meets tragedy first-hand, even though almost everyone can be moved by tragedy. But I doubt whether anyone escapes all the other kinds of unhappiness. There seems to be some crack in us all that lets darkness seep inside.

I think we had all better learn to resist illusion at all times and in all its shapes and shadows; it really is possible to find in this world living centers of loving and trust where one can be happy.

—Ralph Harper

CONTENTS

I
The Experience of Darkness

II
The Darkness of Man

III

The Darkness of God

IV

The Meaning of Darkness

I

The Experience
of Darkness

1

The Country of Darkness

And God divided light from darkness. God called light day, and darkness he called night.—Genesis 1:5

I tried to tell about the night and about the difference between the night and the day and how the night was better unless the day was very clean and cold, and I could not tell it; as I cannot tell it now. But if you have had it, you know. —Hemingway

The Things of the Night

The "things of the night" can be explained in the day, provided "you have had it." This should not mean that if you have had the experience, you do not need the explanation. On the contrary, the deeper and more important the experience, the more urgent the effort to understand. So often we have had experiences and missed their meanings. Sometimes this is because we are too busy and must rush on. Sometimes it is because we are not prepared or are surprised when something new or momentous occurs. Often it is because we are conditioned by society to suppress the fears and terrors of the night. And to some extent we are discouraged from admitting the beauties and the intimacies of night too; we almost never observe any resemblance between night and day.

The night and the day are not the same, that much we know. On the surface we would seem to live mostly in the day. We sleep eight hours and are awake sixteen. But it is not that

3

simple. So much of waking life is depressed by specific anxieties and gnawing, aching premonitions. For that matter, much of each night is a dead loss; and when we do not dream, we do not seem to experience anything at all. Some people never dream, or do not recall their dreams in the morning. Some dreams are lighter than dark; they are happy and fulfilled, unlike the actualities of the day. There is a distinction to be named and insisted on, and yet the overlappings and ambiguities of the symbolism of night and day, darkness and light, are so real that one must be careful not to oversimplify as Hemingway did. Darkness is very close by, at all times.

We are close to darkness every minute of our lives. I do not mean only that we are always just emerging—we hope—from ignorance, and that it takes only a slip or twist to send us back into its shadows. Of course that is so. I mean that our existential confidence, for the sake of which we seek wisdom, is always threatened from inside and from without. When self-confidence wobbles, collapse is near. The pencil's point snaps, the twisted threads unravel against the eye of the needle, the solid squashes, firmness and control quiver and break. We would do almost anything, think almost nothing, to prevent this. Indeed, an undefinable portion of civilized effort goes into keeping us moving so that we will not brood over the flimsiness of our moral or spiritual underpinnings. We settle for almost anything that can keep the line of darkness from advancing across the green.

Some will even humiliate their intelligence to put up with stupidities and evil, and call weakness a virtue. For the most part the victims are unwilling and quite innocent, paschal lambs. Some, like Kierkegaard, we suspect of savoring isolation, seeking melancholy and self-pity. Some, like the poet whom Kierkegaard mentioned, are fated to live in darkness

4

and live only to celebrate it.[1] Suffer again so that your songs will be even sweeter next time! Hard to realize that their poetry is not just a distortion of their pain, but a way of acknowledging the common in the unique. There is a certain beauty in that. They are acquainted with the night, and therefore stand out in front of us, to assure us that darkness is real and that it is not utterly desolate. And so when we are tempted to announce, not without pomposity, that someone must enter the dark, we had better remember that that room is already filled with better men than ourselves.

The Ambiguity of Darkness

We learn the ambiguity of darkness. There is a cold dark, full of fear and loneliness, and a warm dark for embracing and acceptance. There is comfort and security and forgetting in the dark; there is also disorder, crisis, panic. There is panic and there is peace. There is "the dark side of the earth" and "the theoretic bright one."[2] Moreover, in the same person and at the same time we find insight and control on the one hand, and a contrapuntal base of yawning nonbeing on the other.

Darkness has its advantages. It shields us from the distractions of the lighted and peopled rooms, the traffic and the intrusions of all that is not ourselves. The light is out, the house stilled, and stretched or nestled in accustomed sheets we shed abruptly the questions of day and turn with relief to the book of night. "To be continued" arrives all too soon as serialized ruminations falter and sleep blacks us out. But for a few moments the conditions of night are assembled and a doorway crossed. When we stroll along the darkened streets,

[1] *Either-Or* (2 vols.; Princeton, N.J.: Princeton University Press, 1949), I, 15.

[2] *Moby-Dick* (New York: Signet, 1962), p. 495.

unfrightened by the hostile poor, or drive in protective armor to our evening appointments, or walk in country silence broken only by restless birds or far-off highway rumble, as we settle back in the smoky tunnel of a flight across water, we are set free, without being uprooted, from the necessities and distractions of the day; being pushed out from its shores, we venture happily into the welcoming plains of night. Just as the dark of blindness, whether it comes as a temporary result of corrective operations or as a permanent condition, shows one the kindness of other persons, so the recess and breather of the night enables spirit to flow out unhampered, uncensored, innocent.

Whether during night walks or night flights, whether attended by stars and moon, whether air is cold with frost and snow, whether air is warm and tossed with scents of spring, night itself is neutral. Where there is neutrality, the best rushes in to fill the spaces left by bracketed rules and accusations. So are heard voices in the night, whispers in the dark, timid, tentative suggestions of new untried ways. The night is a theater, of the healthy and also of the absurd. For grotesqueness lurks in the dark, violent and ugly, utterly foreign, and once it is met we cannot walk in the dark without fearing evil. And yet there are those who cannot live in the sun, who, accustomed to the protection of night, fear the encroachments and gregariousness of the day. Not for them to see through a glass darkly, but rather to see in the dark more honestly and more surely than under the noon sun's glare.

Sometimes it is good to withdraw from streets and clamor, down the theater aisle to the cushioned privacy of another man's vision of beauty and the absurd. Sometimes it is useful to seek the controlled experience of laughter and sobbing, of a shattered and reassembled world that can appeal to some sense of what really is or what yet may be. While there is time we use artificial darkness to simulate those final moments when, if

6

only in legend, the soul summarizes times and occasions. In the real, final dark the lights are usually kept on. Nurses, relatives, doctors, clergy, go in and out, and wait with scarcely veiled impatience for the anticipated flickering out. In that dark no great judgment, no divine revelation, or, for that matter, no beauty, is allowed to sanctify the sordid seepage of spirit. Those waiting pray treacherously that the night may come, that it may all be over, that the suffering stop or not begin, that life outside may resume. No one expects apocalypse or resurrection, no one expects much wisdom in this night. The end of all our wandering is simple disappearance from the sight of men.

The Many Darknesses

There are many darknesses. There is the darkness of creative solitude and revery. There is the darkness of loving adoration and satisfying supplication and thanksgiving, existential and mystical, human and divine. There is the darkness of tragic suffering and watching, the sudden end of life and hope and virtue. There is the darkness of premonition of evil, depression, and then demoralization. There is the loss of love and the certainty of death. And there is the dark night of the soul, abandoned by God and self and others after the astounding ecstasy of illumination. O happy night, O miserable man!

And life goes on.

> Even the dreadful martyrdom must run its course
> Anyhow in a corner, some untidy spot
> Where the dogs go on with their doggy life
>   and the torturer's horse
> Scratches its innocent behind on a tree.[3]

[3] "Musée des Beaux Arts," *W. H. Auden, A Selection* (Baltimore, Md.: Penguin Books, 1958), p. 61.

And no one knows or cares, or it may seem so. The fact is, life must go on, even for the ones that are left behind after the undertaker and his burden have departed. The preparations must be made, the friends and relatives contacted, the future adjusted.

There is beauty, too, and startling achievement. Cities are rebuilt, planets reached, secrets of the universes of the infinitely small and the infinitely large to be toyed and tampered with. Divisions and prejudices, poverty and want addressed, compassionately and with cold cash and cautious legal justice. All this and more, like the landscape drying on the easel, or the violin concerto reverberating in the mind, allaying fears and tensions, the snow falling, drifts requiring snowshoes, trees enlarged with white. Only a fool forgets that most of the time darkness is experienced in a little hut of one's own while dazzling sunshine plays for miles around.

And yet the night is real, and the things of night too important to be ignored. Someone must tell the truth,[4] describe and estimate the reach of danger, the grip of peril. We need not forget beauty, the morning sun and mist over the lake, accustomed faces and voices. The question is, how do we evaluate them beside death and loss and all finality? Someone must tell the truth about the night, about death and tragedy, friendlessness and demoralization. Someone must ask honestly whether night and day belong to each other or just to the same indifferent world. The answers had better come out of experience and not be the beautiful construction of a mind in fear.

Are we ready for the truth, all of it? Have we really understood so deeply that we will not betray our experience? The truth is that darkness is always near. A man drives his car

---

[4] "It is essential to know the night"; Albert Camus, *The Myth of Sisyphus* (New York: Alfred A. Knopf, 1955), p. 93.

across the wooded hills in a snowstorm. The edges of the road, fence and trees, are dark on either side of the moving prow of the car lights. Within the prow all is bright and shadowless. Outside is nothing, only a landscape remembered from a summer's day. Gradually the wedge fills up with wind and snow, so that nothing can be seen on the outer side of the windshield. We live like that, in the silence on each side of slowdown or swerve and crash. It is easy to forget the enormous effort and fatigue behind the vision and control we call civilization. All it takes is a beautiful snowstorm to subtract it and leave us stranded. Or it could be as if the music downstairs, or a murmuring in another room, or the tapping of wind at the glass should cease being heard in our inner dark, and we be left to ourselves.

Better, of course, a companionable walk with a friend and a dog on a snow-hardened road bordering a dark evergreen wood, better the push and run on a Davos sled at twilight down curving carriage lane to lights and village in the valley. Nietzsche once lived there;[5] how different philosophy might be if he had had a friend he could cling to on a Davos sled. Better a stroll at midnight or at daybreak by fieldstone wall and pink and white dogwood. The darkness tamed, held in check, the grotesque still undiscovered.

Darkness is all too close. So much of our time is spent keeping other people at bay. Perpetually on guard against suspicion, misunderstanding, and accusations, we defend in order to keep control, we attack in order to protect. With so much to lose, we live in constant anxiety lest we be reduced to gibbering. So thin is the membrane separating self-confidence from hysteria, many think it good fortune to seek and find suspended sentence, enjoying their stolidity. But darkness is

[5] Sils Maria.

9

still around them. They do not know how dark the lives of their fellows. Or they are reluctant to admit it. We tell such valiant lies about ourselves to conceal persistent qualms and failures; why should we not suspect in turn that we are not alone?

When darkness comes so close that we do not dare to move on, we have the choice of accepting numbness or reaching out for reassurance. And even when the second option is taken, and motion is resumed, there can always happen moments when darkness thickens and reassurance almost dies. Must we accept insecurity, as an inevitable prospect, from broken trust as far as death itself? Is *insecuritas* so habitual or so natural that it is imprudent to believe it will one day disappear? Do we have any evidence to believe that Mary Magdalen came to the sepulchre of the resurrection "when it was yet dark"?[6] Is the opposite of darkness itself protected by and nourished in darkness?

Illusions in the Dark

There are illusions so sophisticated that it is not cricket to expose them. The heart of man is sometimes so despairing that he will try anything to avoid living in darkness. Let there be light! But who will keep it lit when the lightbringer himself dies? The spectator of tragedy, of someone else's suffering, may experience a purgation of his own feelings of compassion and terror that had united him to a fellow human being and to "the secret cause."[7] But to admit that he was at last purified is a euphemistic way of acknowledging that he had, to protect himself, backed away from both suffering and mystery. And if

[6] The Gospel According to St. John, Chapter 20.

[7] James Joyce, *A Portrait of the Artist as a Young Man* (New York: Compass Books, 1962), p. 204.

10

on top of this the spectator claims to have been elevated, exalted, he is saying, without realizing what he is saying, that he has been using someone else's misery for his own vision or satisfaction. There is no doubt that this is what happens, but can we justify it?

The justification of tragedy does not end there. Those who insist on making moral distinctions between one sufferer and another, one hero and another, between, to be specific, a tragic hero and a pathetic antihero, are usually tempted to call attention to the moral superiority of the actively virtuous man over the frail, neutral one. It is but a short step to rejoicing in the tragic exhibition of wisdom, responsibility, courage, and endurance. This is not to say that virtue should not be admired, and at all times, but to ask whether the "yield" from tragedy should be thought of mainly in terms of a contemplation of virtue any more than in terms of release from almost unbearable compassion and dread.

It is comparatively simple for one who does not suffer, even when he cares for someone who does (and I am thinking now of real as opposed to theatrical tragedy), to back off from the irrational. But that does not make the irrational itself back off. It is easier to pretend that good comes out of evil, that light comes out of darkness. But at what price? And do we have the right to accept this price? Too often men back away from the irrational long before they have really looked it in the face. Joseph Conrad said that no one can stand "naked terror." Perhaps not, but naked terror is not like God; we might at least see it for what it is before announcing that it is harmless.

In religion the dark night of the soul stands for an equally sophisticated temptation. A man spends his life disciplining his mind and heart and actions to conform to the will of God as he understands it. After trials and difficulties he achieves

11

some success, in some instances ecstasy. This is what he was aiming to do. All has gone well. Then one day he founders. God seems to have walked out on him. Ecstasy is followed by depression. He feels deserted by man and God alike, a stranger to everything. But he does not give up. He does not curse God and die. Nor does he become a great sinner. On the contrary, in blankness of mind and with unfeeling heart he goes right on as before. He will not become apostate. Why? Because, say the masters of prayer, he is in God's hands; in fact, his spiritual life has actually taken the final turn toward union with God. All looks dark, but all is really well.

When deserted, why not pull out? Some do. But some do not like to admit that they were on the wrong road all along, and they hold on a little longer. It is consoling to try to believe that they have not been left out in the cold after all. They may be in the right, although their reason speaks more clearly on behalf of emotional needs than of God's presence. Nor is it necessary that disbelief should lead to vice. Too long have believers complacently assumed that they alone live virtuously. True, it is not easy to live in rebellion. But one does not have to; there can be other alternatives to rebellion than faith in God. There can be indifference to God, and also commitment to making and loving in this world and this life.

Nothing is more futile than to dispute the facts of darkness. Why try to explain away the end of the finite, death and desertion? They happen. And long before we encounter ultimate solitude and the shutdown of consciousness, we are besieged and battered by snubs and recriminations, bewilderment and failure, sickness and frustration, numbness and despair. Over against our really huge ignorance we light feeble candles that flicker and sometimes go out. It takes all the energy and

12

nerve we are born with to keep relighting them. A man loses his job, a woman her husband or her child, a child is ignored by his parents. How many times during life can one experience failure and yet survive as a functioning organism? Even when one does not cry, "Why me?" but patiently takes blow on blow, a day comes when nerves can take no more.

Images of Darkness

As at a party when one suddenly feels like screaming, "Let me out!" how many grown men and women have wanted to run away from home and job, wanted to run away and be forgotten? There are times when what has been built up no longer seems worth holding on to or keeping in check.

There are even times when one no longer knows whether he believes anything at all. Sometimes the more a man knows, the less easy it is to believe anything. We choose our lives, and life becomes a trap that only the brave or the irresponsible can extricate themselves from.

How many have waked up in the morning exhausted from having seen the clock face every half hour until five o'clock, when something gave way and consciousness finally was shut down until time to get up? Then, fears still unresolved, one is too worn out to care.

Some people try and try to succeed in something important to them, and the result is failure. After so much trying they come to believe they are made for failure.

Others try to talk to God. They really try. They have read that saints have got through to Him and that anyone can become a saint if he tries. They seem to have been misinformed, hearing nothing but the beating of their own hearts and the rain on the porch roof.

13

Many say that they find solace in friendship. Not everyone can. Each time they anticipate real presence, and each time they are let down.

Once upon a time a young man left his town to seek employment in a big city. As the train left the yards, past the sooty walls of underpasses, he felt defenseless and vulnerable, almost desperate. Where was he going? Why was he on this train? Would it not be better to put up with life at home rather than journey into this unknown? Later, when he had learned to endure much unease, he still felt nostalgia like seasickness. *Insecuritas*—that compound of habitual melancholy, geographical displacement, and metaphysical solitude—surged through him from head to toe. He had heard that it is not the worst as long as you can say it is the worst. This was confirmed the night he put up at a hotel near an airport, and was wrenched into intense semiconsciousness, a fraction of a second ahead of the scream of a jet as it zeroed in on his room through the open balcony. He got ready in that second of seconds to assimilate the scream into his body, provided he could resist the tearing apart of his nerves long enough. The plane passed over the hotel.

Outside the wind kept trying to come in. He gave it his attention. What was it trying to say? Occasionally he thought he might be hearing something new. But he could not be sure until he had heard it again. Once in a while something dreamed of really happened, and then later it seemed only a dream. He was not sure, but it did seem once or twice that he had seen or heard something, sometime, somewhere, more real than all he had ever told or thought.

II

The Darkness
of Man

2

A Spectrum of Darkness

Why art thou so full of heaviness, O my soul?—Psalm 42

A Structure and a Sequence

Happy the man who can say he does not know black darkness. In fact, most civilized people have not personally experienced either the darkness of tragedy or the dark night of the soul. These experiences are, as it were, special cases outside the ordinary run of life. But is there anyone who does not know melancholy? Even if there is, to be spared by fate or insulated by an easy-going nature, would not necessarily be an advantage. There is much to be learned, let alone endured, in suffering. On the one hand, we would be lucky if we did not have cause to suffer or could endure it wisely and with equanimity. On the other hand, whatever threatens also indirectly calls attention to our hopes. The limitations of human nature and chance must be faced without illusion, so that we can develop without shutting ourselves off from reality. The person who pretends that conflicts can be avoided, is as immature as one who makes a point of getting along with fools and knaves.

At the other extreme are those burdened with a melancholic disposition. They unfailingly see all the evidence for a negative view of life, and unless they are deranged they generally tell the truth. It is their weighing of the evidence that is often questionable. They will usually look out for and unerringly find the most damaging facts, which will in one instance turn

17

out to be significant, and in another instance turn out to be irrelevant. They can be counted on to vote "no" every time; but someone else should decide the validity of the ballot. They usually give themselves and others a bad time. But they cannot be ignored, not only because they speak in good faith, but because they are apt to be more sensitive than other people, and are needed to correct others' complacency.

Under cover of darkness much goes on that would be better avoided or forgotten, many evils planned or done. In the same darkness the world outside seems remote and unattainably unreal. Whoever would understand the feelings of darkness must enter it one way or another. A psychiatrist or a pastor does this vicariously in order to promote and restore unobstructed functioning in others. Psychiatrists and pastors deal with exceptions, at least to the extent that anyone who asks for help is an exception. But anyone whose tolerance of the dark side of life has weakened, so that he cannot go about his business, does need help. Melancholy may seem too unpleasant to be thought about by those who are not interested in mental health. Unfortunately, melancholia is not atypical, but rather a state known to some degree by everyone.

Few realize that melancholia has both structure and sequence. There is not one melancholy, but many. Without being dogmatic or exclusive, it is safe to say that the various feelings that would be called melancholic probably fall into half a dozen classes. And these represent a deepening of sadness, from initial boredom and restlessness to complete demoralization, the outer bounds of the spectrum, the colors of darkness. Within the spectrum each color, so to speak, has its self-definition, its view of reality, and its outlet. We can ask four questions about our feelings. How do I feel? What does the world look like? What am I likely to do? Why do I feel like this?

18

The last question is sometimes very difficult to answer. So often melancholy is too overwhelming to allow the question even to be asked. Nothing is more oppressive than a negative feeling. Michelangelo Antonioni has said, "I am positive that the world today is filled more with dead feelings than with live ones. I would like to know more about these residues."[1] Through him we can. But the spectrum is even more diverse than he imagines, and because he is an artist rather than a philosopher he has not tried to find its structure.

Probably Dostoevsky was the first to do this. His novels can be read as case-books of melancholia, compared to which Kierkegaard's repetitious references (except for his analysis of certain forms of despair in *Sickness unto Death*) to his own melancholy are thin and superficial. Dostoevsky's descriptions and discussions are still unexcelled both in scope and in penetration. He knew melancholy first-hand. And melancholy has to be known that way. Otherwise the analyst or the writer may miss something that is felt by the sufferer. Nevertheless Dostoevsky has not left us with an ordered spectrum, only a series of renderings of its colors. The classification we must make ourselves. Each of us, therefore, starts from scratch, prompted by personal as well as vicarious experience, by nature and by art, by philosophy and by psychology. To tell the truth, even textbooks on psychiatry are not very helpful, even by way of providing descriptions of feelings that are common enough to justify systematic presentation.

For those who are inclined to pass off problems of melancholia as dispositions inherited by some individuals and not by others, e.g., a Kierkegaard or a Virginia Woolf, a corrective is

---

[1] *Screenplays of Michelangelo Antonioni* (New York: The Orion Press, 1963), p. xii.

in order. Kierkegaard called it "the defect of our age."[2] And so, whenever one is convinced that Kierkegaard was preoccupied with melancholy because he was born unhappy (and he was the first to admit this) we might ask whether there is anything in his conviction, and Dostoevsky's, that modern times promote melancholy. Even after acknowledging that the causes of melancholy in figures of Russian fiction in the nineteenth century are different from the causes of melancholy in the middle of this century, we may recognize a pervasive metaphysical instability common to both centuries. This instability has expressed itself in several ways, in social upheavals as well as in religious and moral questioning. But behind these phenomena lies the image of lost faith and a lost God. No one saw this more clearly than Nietzsche. It has been left to us to feel the consequences. We are now in a position to see what they are, and to see them in some intelligible sequence.

Boredom

Boredom (*ennui*) is not a modern psychological phenomenon. Bernanos, like Pascal before him, was not far wrong in calling it "the true condition of man."[3] The desert fathers called it *acedia* (*accidie*); the medieval contemplatives called it aridity, dryness. St. Augustine, and Pascal, knew it as disquietude; we know it as restlessness, unease. These two words have different values, of course. Restlessness is more energetic; unease is heavier and also more vague. Both are mobile in comparison with the lassitude, listlessness, inertia, apathy, and torpor that are sometimes used to define tedium and boredom. Boredom is not a single feeling, but a complex of feelings. It is a state signifying a withdrawal from life, and it

[2] *Either-Or*, II, 20.

[3] *The Diary of a Country Priest* (New York: Image Books, 1956), p. 2.

may be registered in restlessness or its opposite, apathy. But the apathy is to be distinguished from the apathy of exhaustion. In that state apathy is the effect of fatigue, and cannot be dealt with directly. In boredom apathy can vanish in a flash when the person finds some reason to take an interest in life again.

The bored man sees no reason to move. But his inertia is not to be thought of as permanent; it can slip so easily into restlessness. He can pull himself together, at least to the extent of taking a malicious swipe at the world. When bored a person temporarily loses his reason to act or to care, he can be saved only by novelty and diversion, as Pascal so well understood. Some will seek diversion; others will expect to be diverted, and will obstinately refuse to take measures themselves. It is said that only the idle are bored. But like many other popular sayings, it is not true, and throws little light on the causes. Many active, responsible persons are bored, and force themselves to keep busy, not so much to stave off boredom as to stave off despair.

"Why art thou so full of heaviness, O my soul? And why art thou so disquieted within me?" Because the soul has lost its motive, and is no longer able to make enthusiastic use of the accepted values of its environment. It knows them too well, and is bored by them. Those who uncritically accept the world as handed out are generally less sensitive or care less for their freedom of choice. One may envy those who say, "I am never bored," but not because "there is always so much to do," but because their energy and equanimity reflect a serious view of life. They are not as liable to be victims of the general instability of public values.

To the bored the world may seem flat, grotesque, violent. From Kafka's *Metamorphosis* to Beckett's *Waiting for Godot*

21

to Antonioni's *Blow-up* we now have many illustrations of this theme. Violence is part of the structure of boredom. In some measure the grotesque reveals the feeling the bored man has about the indifference and the impartial violence around him. So much more happens; there are so many more people all the time, so many more ideas and refinements of ideas, that impersonality seems to express the nature of the individual as well as the character of his environment. And, in spite of the principles and organizations of order in society, violence has become more diverse and more unpredictable. Is it any wonder that the grotesque is a feature of modern life?

What can be done about boredom? The spirit of man remains empty, in suspension, marking time, not because it is unable to concentrate, resolve, choose, act, but rather because it sees nothing worth choosing. There is nothing interesting left. And yet, as occasional fits of restlessness show, boredom comes not at the end of the road, but at the beginning. There is enough energy left to be used in occasional exercises. The extreme case of Dostoevsky's Stavroguin[4] is instructive, although not typical. Stavroguin could be cold and immobile (his face a mask) one moment, and gay or cruel the next, with no apparent reason for the transformation. The change from inertia to a motiveless freedom solves nothing; the last state will soon be worse than the first.

A personality transformation, spontaneous or deliberate (as with Stavroguin), is always a possibility. Without habitual psychic activity the self will lose its moral habit of resolution and become dangerously inert. If the self cannot act, it can still dream, and one way out is to make-believe a world, fantastic or grotesque, in which the perspective of boredom

[4] Feodor Dostoevsky, *The Possessed.*

22

can be mirrored. This can free the spirit, not merely by putting it to work, but by giving it significant work. What is more meaningful to a bored person than the creation of a world like his own which he has never experienced? Fight fire with fire? No, fight the worn-out given with the new creation. Not only will invention seem livelier than the world as handed out, the new in the familiar will call attention to the truth about the familiar for the first time. In the end reality will seem as strange and as interesting as fiction.

The most common example of melancholy man is the bored man. Nineteenth-century fiction, particularly Russian fiction, is full of bored men, from Pechorin[5] and Eugene Onegin[6] to the Underground Man[7] and Stavroguin. But just as there are two kinds of boredom, immobile and restless, so there are two consequences, numbness and dreaming. While there is restlessness, there is hope; the dreamer, although bored or frustrated in his waking life, is young in spirit in his dream life. His dreams may be night-dreams or day-dreams. He himself is young, in the sense of immature. When boredom takes the form of numbness, when the bored man becomes unfeeling, cold, indifferent to the welfare of others, he is potentially dangerous to society. He is dangerous to himself as well, for his sense of motive and his self-control may degenerate rapidly, skipping other possible stages of darkness, until he becomes depressed or demoralized. There is no guarantee that even in the descent into deeper darkness one will pass neatly and in good order from stage to stage. The soul may sink rapidly from its own heaviness.

[5] Mikhail Yurevich Lermontov, *A Hero of Our Time.*
[6] Aleksandr Sergeyevich Pushkin, *Eugene Onegin.*
[7] Dostoevsky, *Notes from Underground.*

Suffocation

Stamina is a mystery. You either have it or you do not. And if you do not, you can do something, although not much, to pretend you do. Each person is born, apparently, with a certain tolerance of stress, to take so much and no more. Pressure builds up. Sooner or later anyone will break. Just as no one knows the day of his death, so no one knows how much pressure—and too much boredom can act as a pressure too—it will take to crack him wide open.

Pressure by itself is not always an enemy. Sometimes it is tension, a tearing apart, a twisting and pulling, together with more intense consciousness and concentration. The damage may be located in the frustration rather than the challenge, obstacles of one sort or another blocking each attempt to break through. If so, then it is easier to understand what boredom and pressure have in common. Each can end in suffocation and in explosion. The bored man can live with boredom only so long. Then he becomes fed up. He can take no more. He wants out. He cannot breathe. He gasps, chokes, screams. Whether he loses his breath or whether he releases his anger, he is trying to smash the walls around him. He feels surrounded by a world that now looks too trivial to bother with—or hostile, or meaningless. It is not meant for him, and has nothing for him. And so there is mutual rejection. "The best lack all conviction; while the worst are full of passionate intensity."[8] "Panic and emptiness . . . telegrams and anger!"[9] The self sees itself surrounded by meaningless people leading meaningless lives which they are too stupid or mean to feel. It

[8] W. B. Yeats, "The Second Coming," *The Collected Poems of W. B. Yeats* (London: Macmillan & Co. Ltd., 1955), p. 210.

[9] E. M. Forster, *Howards End* (New York: Vintage Books, 1962), pp. 26–27.

is eroded by the snobbery of the rich and the meanness of the genteel poor, the busy complacency of the in-betweens. All seem bent, as Pascal prophesied, on ignoring both light and darkness. And when the darkness of this world is challenged by knights of faith, crusaders for justice and creativity, the others shrink back into their dull preserves. Resenting any attempt to observe real gradations of value in individual human beings and individual works of art, "the crowd" finds its identity and security in the conventions of its friends. Mindless chatter is as useful as inimitable reflection, both taken as hedges against the dark cloud of death over the hills.

In such a world how can one be honest or sincere, to say nothing of being wise and resolute? For most men it is not possible. Their tolerance of black darkness is not great enough. General instability in an age like ours, added to the personal frustrations and failures normal in any lifetime, almost excuse courting oblivion. Only the sensitive—the weak as well as the strong—survive this siege, but usually not for long. Whether death is long or slow in coming, it comes surely, although not necessarily through suffocation or explosion. Some are reserved for other and darker fates, death by paralysis or fragmentation. Only a few survive, snatching themselves or being snatched from the shadowed well at some level of the spiral plunge.

Exhaustion

Life takes its toll of psychic energies. After forty, men are candidates for heart attacks, after sixty for strokes. The physical damage is incalculable. The success of prevention and healing is also hard to count on. But despite the shaking up, in many instances the patient returns to life without feeling his values permanently altered. He learns quickly to adjust to the expectations of other people and to his own habits. But it does not work out so easily with emotional structures that crack; subconsciously they provide their own slowdown in order to avoid fragmentation. In addition, there is a difference between the building up of tension and pressure and the gradual draining of motive and purpose. There is a difference between nervous tension and nervous exhaustion; the former cannot be tolerated after a certain point by mind or body, while the latter may simply reduce the functioning of will and intellect to the place where it is physically secure but emotionally dead.

There is nothing more exhausting than struggling to keep one's integrity intact through years of frustration, and the buffeting and assaults of misunderstanding. Exhaustion is largely the result of prolonged defensive action. It is not the successful who wear out emotionally, but the unsuccessful. No one knew this better than Scott Fitzgerald, whose own life and fiction are such clear witnesses to this contemporary disease. For disease it is, when spirit is chronically tired. A lesion of vitality, or emotional exhaustion, can advance to the point where effort, even desire, is not able to undertake any course that must run through several stages. Desire may be too weak to plan, and will too weak to achieve, and the will collapses almost as soon as it stirs. After a few attempts the self may stop trying, convinced that it is too powerless to sustain itself. The worst thing is the realization that now nobody else is to blame. Frustration has become built-in, an emotional habit immune to motive. "It was strange to have no self—to be like a little boy left alone in a big house, who knew that now he could do anything he wanted to do, but found there was nothing he wanted to do."[10]

[10] F. Scott Fitzgerald, *The Crack-Up* (New York: New Directions, 1962), p. 79.

The more exhausted a person becomes, the more indifferent he is to the world around him, even that part of it which seems to threaten him. The world becomes a blank, a two-dimensional screen on which someone else has scrawled meaningless lines. Noises are far away. When they call, he responds apathetically. He no longer cares whether they are meant for him. Likewise, the integrity of the self, which he had jealously, angrily fought for through the years, no longer interests him. He has become resigned to being a nobody.

Emotional exhaustion is a worse state by far than either boredom or suffocation. The bored or suffocated at least commonly have in reserve their alter-egos of restlessness and anger to save them from complete torpor. The bored man can still dream and create; the person who cannot stand any more mediocrity can always blow up, strike out at the world. He is not sick, not drained of energy needed for movement and change. Emotional exhaustion, on the other hand, is a dangerous state to be in. The intellect remains lucid but the will is too sluggish to sustain action. Even with a little self-control left intact, the spirit is to all practical purposes dead. It is not surprising, therefore, that the remaining energy is sometimes channeled into desperate acts of defiance or into self-defeating indulgence.

Bad as this is, there is worse. For some who are emotionally exhausted, the slowdown prevents the self from fully realizing its loss of opportunity. These persons do not suffer as intensely as those who feel the more restless forms of *acedia*. Like them, they have not arrived at the place of immobility or complete loss of control. Like them, they hope that a new beginning can still be made. But it cannot be made without help. Someone must intervene. Some new opportunity must be offered, or, at the very least, recognition and encouragement given. Com-

27

pared to what the truly depressed spirit requires, the degree of help needed to bring about a transformation is minimum. The world itself will not have to be reassessed. Emotional exhaustion is not caused by a loss of faith, and does not need a new commitment. What it does require is rest in order to conserve its remaining energies, give time for recuperation and growth. The time may come when exhaustion fades and boredom returns. This is not an ideal or a pleasant alternative, but it does hold promise of a revival of will power and the restoration of normal if not creative efforts.

Despondency

There is a state of mind—call it despondency, dejection, *tristitia*—which is so close to emotional exhaustion that it is sometimes taken for it. Indeed, those whose exhaustion responds to sympathy and recognition pass through periods of discouragement that leave them limp. But their lethargy is not the definitive feature of their condition. Rather it is loss of belief in themselves, and of their power to act so that they will be judged worthy by others. They feel despondent because they feel rejected. Despondency is a crisis of identity. The anonymity that they suffer from is caused, in their view, by their being too unimportant or just too unlucky to be noticed. Since no one else pities them, they pity themselves. And when they get sympathy they must respond quickly and effectively so as to capture the passing recognition that they think they deserve,

Anna Karenina noticed one day how many streets and houses were filled with people she would never know, whose lives were as full of anxieties as her own. This is an emotional acknowledgment of a fact that at other times makes no impression at all. We do not know them, and they do not know us.

28

Life passes us by; we are unknown, unrecognized, uncared for. At times one is brushed by a discouragement so heavy that it feels as if the interior walls of one's frame were being sucked together, and it is difficult to stand upright. This is what lends authority to failure, this and the thought and belief that are put into a job which turns out to be useless. This lesion of identity, of belief in one's work and oneself, is far more serious than the lesion of energy and enthusiasm of the *homme épuisé.*" Many more human beings than would be supposed suffer silently and out of sight over their failure to be recognized and their failure to believe in their work. Discouragement may not numb or kill, but it is for that reason all the harder to bear. And if it persists, it can lead to depression.

Depression and Demoralization

The four levels of darkness already discussed are still within sight of the daylight coming down the shaft. A person at one of those levels is not as helpless or as solitary as one who suffers from depression and demoralization. Ingmar Bergman says that the third smile of a summer night is "for the sad, the depressed, the sleepless, the confused, the frightened, the lonely."[11] They, unlike the bored and the dejected, cannot easily hide; we know their number as legion. They become burdens to others, and sometimes, partly out of pride, take themselves out of the way of others permanently because their burden is too great for anyone to carry. Virginia Woolf felt herself to be one of these. One of the favored few of our time, she brought into the world "a great lake of melancholy,"[12] "a

[11] *Four Screenplays* (New York: Simon and Schuster, 1960), p. 94; cf. Chapter 4, n.23.
[12] *A Writer's Diary* (London: Hogarth, 1965), p. 140; cf. Chapter 3, n.8.

wedge-shaped core of darkness."[13] "Some inner loneliness"[14] at times rose up and overwhelmed all her instinct for work and enjoyment. At these times she felt like saying, "I shall make myself face the fact that there is nothing . . . nothing for any of us."[15]

Virginia Woolf's melancholy, her depression, was an inherited flaw in her being. We cannot learn to escape her particular darkness. But, however arrived at, depression feels the same to everyone. It is amazing how similar are the descriptions of the relatively small number of emotional stages that a man can pass through. But for the person who is not temperamentally inclined to suffer from depressive states, the cause of depression will be some great, specific loss, whether of person or meaning, and the results will be loneliness and despair. The cause is sometimes subjective, hard to trace, a sense of life as empty and useless. St. Augustine sent his concubine back to North Africa, and his "heart which clung to her was broken and wounded and dripping blood."[16] He did not remain depressed for long; he had to make history. Henry Adams grieved for his dead wife and their lost happiness for thirty years afterwards. But that did not prevent him from writing about history and himself. "What a vast fraternity it is—that of 'hearts that ache'. For the last three months it has seemed to me as though all society were coming to me, to drop its mask for a moment and initiate me into the mystery. How we do suffer! And we go on laughing; for, as a practical joke at our expense, life is a success."[17]

[13] *To the Lighthouse* (New York: Harcourt, Brace & Co., 1955), p. 95.
[14] *A Writer's Diary*, p. 147.
[15] *Ibid.*, p. 144.
[16] *The Confessions of St. Augustine*, trans. Rex Warner (New York: Mentor Books, 1963), p. 133.
[17] *Letters of Henry Adams*, to Henry Holt, March 8, 1886 (Boston: Houghton Mifflin Co., 1938).

St. Augustine and Henry Adams endured. Both were helped by friends, and both had unusually strong professional interests to distract them, for Augustine his quest for God, for Henry Adams, his quest for a pattern in history. Neither seems to have reached the place of ultimate solitude experienced by Virginia Woolf. "I wonder how a year or so perhaps is to be endured . . . the inane pointlessness of all this existence . . . the old treadmill feeling of going on and on and on for no reason."[18] Writing seemed to help, but the time came when it no longer helped and she chose to die. Her life had become absolutely dark, and before losing all control she decided to use her will in one last meaningful act, suicide.

In recurrent depressions a man may reach a level of darkness which seems to be permanent. But by definition it is not. Its character is suspension rather than immobility, however immobile it may appear. While there is life there is hope. More accurately, while there are other people there is hope. There are, it is true, degrees of depression. The higher degrees can be endured, and beyond apparent endurance some people themselves find ways of lifting themselves out of extreme heaviness of soul. They know themselves well enough to recognize the symptoms, "the same fluttering in the stomach, the same restlessness, the yawning,"[19] then the feeling of loss, usually indefinite, and finally the specter of despair. This "threat of non-being" (in Paul Tillich's phrase), ranging through degrees of emptiness and meaninglessness, can be observed from inside with detached concern. Darkness is not by any means impenetrable.

In fact, it is not impossible to feel that depression provides one with an opportunity to understand what he usually does

---

[18] *A Writer's Diary*, p. 180.

[19] C. S. Lewis, *A Grief Observed* (Greenwich, Conn.: Seabury Press, 1963), p. 7.

not understand as he stumbles along through life. Virginia Woolf saw this too. "Directly I stop working I feel that I am sinking down, down. And as usual I feel that if I sink further I shall reach the truth."[20] What truth? That is hard to say. For it is like the dreams that introduce us to the heart of some mystery, but which we cannot remember when we awaken. Perhaps the explanation for this illusion is that longing has been substituted for lost possessions by a psychic organism that depends for functioning on some measure of faith. Without a reality that one can depend on, the mind of man has to close down. The last chance it has to go on without outside help is to imagine a truth which can be discovered at the bottom of the pit. Pathetic? Yes, but also not without hope, as it reveals a last desperate effort to restore hope.

Two other alternatives are present in a depressive state. The first and more obvious is immobility. The distant world going about its business as usual is no longer heard. The self stares out unseeing and uncaring. It may not be reached by all the care and ingenuity in the world. Whatever the cause—the withholding or the withdrawal of love, self-confidence, the disappearance of meaning, or God, or some pathological flaw—the result is the same, a withdrawal beyond self-motivation to iron immobility.

The second alternative represents a way out of depression, but also another and final level of darkness. Virginia Woolf's understanding of herself can help us here. Her description of a nervous breakdown as the refusal of some part of the mechanism suggests a fragmentation of what in a depressive state is still a whole. A person suffering from depression is at least preserved from demoralization. It is arguable whether one

[20] *A Writer's Diary*, p. 144.

state is worse than the other. Which is worse, marking time or running wild? Which is worse, not caring or not knowing? Which is worse, regret or fear? Which is worse, waiting indefinitely or striking out in all directions aimlessly? In either case the place is hell, "the outer darkness"[21] reserved for the callous and the cruel. Part of this hell comes from not deserving to be sent there. The depressed have not withdrawn— although this is how they are sometimes described; meaning has withdrawn from them. Whether slowly or from shock of some sudden loss, reality has lost definition, and they feel abandoned. As a result, having lost their bearings they then can lose control as well.

When a person reaches the point where he no longer knows anything for sure, he has reached the inmost room of the house of darkness. When he sees everything that he was once sure of now in flux, convictions dissolved and facts blurred, arrangements in kaleidoscopic motion, glance here, glance there, he can find no place to rest his mind, and therefore no reason to commit himself to anything. When the mind's sense of order fades into disorder, truth is the first victim. There is no truth. There is no contact. Control is impossible. In the middle of speaking, confusion; in the course of feeling or thinking, chaos. Minor hysteria, just contained, threatens to turn into a scream as the heart records the withdrawal of common sense and memory. This is demoralization, a veritable "darkness at noon."[22]

Long before a person reaches this terminus he has been beset night after night, whether asleep or awake, by unresolved

[21] Matthew 25:30.

[22] Arthur Koestler's *Darkness at Noon*; title taken from the time of the Crucifixion: "from the sixth hour there was darkness over all the land unto the ninth hour" (Matthew 27:45).

33

despair. Fear, recurrent, wavelike, holds him relentlessly under. Or, like malaria, the fear returns after a season of respite: "Well, do you have an answer for me this time? I'm not going to give you much more time." And so "fears and terrors of the night,"[23] "darkling fears,"[24] roll in like sea fog and the self begins to drown. Things lose their proportion. The self no longer knows what matters and what does not, what is trivial and what is important. "At three o'clock in the morning a forgotten package has the same tragic importance as a death sentence . . . and in a really dark night of the soul it is always three o'clock in the morning, day after day."[25] The travails of the night are unimpeachable. "Hold them cheap may who ne'er hung there."[26] And if the travail of the night does not exhaust self, spending self to vapor, if "night more and more surrounds me,"[27] the night may become continuous with the day. Then Gethsemane becomes indistinguishable from the "darkness at noon."

Everyone has his own darkness. It becomes part of his lot in life and part of his personality, to be put up with rather than understood. Moods, habitual or recurrent, have this character, and we accept them without feeling that we must understand their philosophical implications. In this way emotional darkness is quite different from tragedy. The tragic sufferer will never be the same again, and yet the difference is very likely to be hidden from the eyes of others. He will be changed inside, at a level of understanding that does not affect his common

[23] Seventh-century Latin hymn; *The Hymnal of The Protestant Episcopal Church*, No. 164.

[24] Sixth-century Latin hymn; *ibid.*, No. 163.

[25] Fitzgerald, *The Crack-Up*, p. 75.

[26] G. M. Hopkins, *Poems and Prose of Gerard Manley Hopkins*, selected by W. H. Gardner (Baltimore, Md.: Penguin Books, 1962), No. 42.

[27] Nietzsche, Letter to Franz Overbeck, February 1883.

sense, and that does not prevent him from carrying on the business of life as before. After a time of assimilation he will seem to be the same old man, even at times to himself.

Not so the person under the influence of one of the moods or modes of emotional darkness. His boredom will show. His impatience will be noticed. One minute he will seem sluggish, the next, on edge. When worn out, he will not respond. When despondent, discouraged, he will not hear. When depressed, he will seem absent. When demoralized, he will make others fear. He will be known, in each mode, according to the change wrought in his personality by his acquaintance with some color of darkness.

The tragic sufferer is more alone than anyone. Fate has isolated him, made him an existential solitary, outside the bounds of the ideal and the probable. It is natural for him to ask for compassion and be given it. In most modes of emotional darkness the self experiences an entirely different kind of solitude, one in which the sufferer feels so far removed from the moods of those around him that it would seem irrelevant and useless to appeal for help. Seldom is the cry, "What shall I do, answer me, answer me," heard; and when it is, the plight behind it seems either too vague or too complex to be answered. Where does one begin? What, after all, is it all about? All of life has gone into the making of a mood. How can a new life be begun when the old life is still largely unknown? We would say, "I am sorry," except that this seems so trivial, so unfeeling. We would say, "I understand," except that we do not. We would say, "Come to me, and I will help and comfort," except that this cannot happen. So men and women are condemned to live in cold shadows which, as they deepen, conceal them from the sight of each other. As darkness hides one from another, the psychic heat drops. As understanding

35

and trust thin out and finally disappear, the warmth essential for human life cools. As the warmth of one, then another, then another, fades, the very condition of life is transformed. Total darkness, a time of ice, is on the way.

Death

Total darkness is death, not just in symbol but in fact. We "beings-unto-death" can never quite forget this sure prospect, no matter how hard we try. It gets nearer every minute, inexorably nearer. A child can suddenly become a full human being when for the first time he has the intuition of his own end. Nothing will be the same again. He knows that sometime he will feel the ice himself, and that there will come "darkness and the shadow of death."[28] Pascal's line is the classical image of inexorableness: "Let us imagine a number of men in chains, and all condemned to death . . . it is an image of the condition of men."[29] Apart from the foreboding apprehension of death, the unknown has always been expressed simply in terms of the darkness that we do know. Homer, in the *Iliad*, again and again uses this image: "A mist of darkness closed over both eyes."[30] "A covering of black night came over both eyes."[31] "The hateful darkness closed in about him."[32] Death is the seventh and final color of the spectrum.

So unthinkable is total darkness and death that man will not—not cannot—conceive this darkness without some light. For the Christian, Christ, light of the world, has given light "to

[28] Psalm 107:10.

[29] *Pensées* (New York: E. P. Dutton, 1954), par. 199.

[30] *The Iliad of Homer*, trans. Richmond Lattimore (Chicago: Phoenix Books, 1962), p. 127.

[31] *Ibid.*, p. 136.

[32] *Ibid.*, p. 289.

them that sit in darkness [*tenebrae*] and in the shadow of death."[33] "Vanquisher of darkness,"[34] his resurrection is type and promise of the deliverance from the darkness of the grave. Even those who are not sure of this will imagine, like Tolstoy, in thinking of death, "the black sack . . . the black hole,"[35] that at the bottom of the sack or hole is light. Falling rapidly from boredom through depression and demoralization, so swiftly that there is no time to savor separately the diversity of melancholy, a man readies himself for the final drop. "Out went the candle, and we were left darkling."[36] Death does not usually arrive in such methodical progression, but at a time when it is not expected, and when a man may be surrounded by more love than ever before. This love may outlast him, and for some that is enough.

[33] Luke 1:79.

[34] Venantius Fortunatus, *The Hymnal of the Protestant Episcopal Church*, No. 87.

[35] *The Death of Ivan Ilych*, trans. Louise and Aylmer Maude (London: Oxford University Press, 1957), p. 71.

[36] Shakespeare, *King Lear*, Act I, scene iv, line 208.

3

Tragedy

How thin a casing protects our life against being devoured from without and disorganized within. A breath and the skiff splits and founders; a nothing and all is imperilled; a cloud and all is darkness. . . . As long as one averts one's eyes from this implacable reality, the tragedy of life is hidden; the moment one looks it in the face, the true proportions of all things are restored.—Henri Frederic Amiel

A bored man is not tragic, nor is tragedy boring. And if *ennui* were the only form of melancholy, then tragedy could hardly be considered side by side with it. Besides, *ennui* is an emotional state, and tragedy an action. The effects of the action on participants and onlookers may be various, but boredom is not one of them. Tragedy is too frightening for that. But even the tragic hero can feel suffocated, exhausted, depressed, and demoralized, although he would hardly be called a hero—rather only a victim—if that were all one could say of his reaction to what had hit him.

Is there any good reason to consider tragedy side by side with the spectrum of melancholy, aside from the obvious deep unhappiness that they share? There is, and the reason is that whether it is an emotional state or tragedy that one is concerned with, the concern is mainly with the causes of unhappiness. We want to know what has happened and why. We ask what is wrong when we feel depressed, and we mean by that, what are the causes of the feeling of depression. When fate and freedom lock horns, and someone suffers irremediably, we ask

38

why did it happen. And we soon discover that while we can find out why we are depressed, we never find a satisfactory answer to justify the pile-driving action of fate. Indeed, the desperate man may be led to realize in either case that more important by far than the answers to his cries about causation, is the search for a way out, or a way to survive—morally, spiritually—and the courage to take it.

One thing more: tempting as it always is for the mind that would systematize, it would probably be a mistake to try to see the ghost of God, dead or alive, behind either tragic suffering or any of the colors of melancholy. Of course, the discovery of God's presence would make all the difference to both tragic hero and onlooker, to the depressed and the chronically fatigued. "Come unto me, all ye that travail and are heavy laden, and I will refresh you."[1] But we know enough not to expect that, and we cannot insist or insinuate. There are, however, special cases where the emotional effect of the experience of God's silence can be depressing or demoralizing (but hardly boring or suffocating or exhausting), and similarly for some men life could become irremediably disastrous if it turned out that for them God was dead. God has mattered that much to some of our contemporaries, and his loss has been as overwhelming as the loss of a person has been to others; or, to put it more accurately, it is tragic when a man discovers that out of his very zeal for truth he has killed the God who used to be Truth. It is like participating innocently in the death of one's father.

Tragic Reversal

The mark of tragedy is its reversal of everything one ordinarily takes for granted. This is obvious. What is not obvious is how much one does take for granted. Even if we live on the

[1] Matthew 11:28.

illusion that life will go on and on indefinitely, we know that it will not: no one is really so foolish as to believe himself beyond change and death. But it is extraordinary how much we know and how little we show. We have an almost infinite trust in things as they are, going on and on. Night follows morning, bedtime, sleep, dreaming, waking, shaving, eating breakfast, thinking, talking, walking, driving, and so on. Our sense of real expectation is unshakable, and it is stuffed with a gaggle of habits. Many of them bore us, and yet we feel secure with them. We welcome pleasant surprises, of course, and prefer not to remember that unpleasant surprises may also come our way. Professional pessimists may talk and moan about anticipated ills, but we notice that the pessimists are just as unprepared and just as shocked when they too are hurt. Nobody is ever really prepared for tragedy. We might say that if someone were, it would not be tragedy. Joseph K., in Kafka's *The Trial,* says complacently, "It is only a trial if I recognize it as such."[2] The trouble is, tragedy has a way of overwhelming both complacency and defiance.

Tragedy is the suffering that convinces man that life is not to be taken for granted. In a sense, then, ordinary life is a reprieve from real life. Perhaps it seems like playing with words, but real life means possible life, what can happen, despite our wishes, caution, preparations, routines, our illusion that we have it made. The method of the reprieve is illusion. For what else can we call a state of mind in which one is brainwashed to ignore disaster? We are always on the edge of tragedy, every single man, woman, and child. If we could take this in, it is doubtful that we would continue complacently with life as we now know it. Most people simply do not realize this until forced.

[2] New York: Modern Library, 1956, p. 51.

Comedy, on the other hand, enables man to live with his illusions. In comedy suffering is not taken seriously, no one really gets hurt; at least we are not meant to care. And so life, being accepted, is enhanced. The ground does not threaten to open up. We will not be swallowed alive; we will touch life lightly at all bases. Comedy is, on the whole, more honest than we are. When we laugh we no longer pretend that life is not to be feared. On the contrary, we laugh because we know well that we may have to cry tomorrow. Comedy is not meant to reinforce illusion, but to strengthen the human being who feels unprotected by illusion. Comedy may use the stuff of ordinary life, but it is an antidote to the boredom that shadows ordinary life, as well as a tranquilizer for disquietude and foreboding.

Comedy can strengthen sanity prior to tragedy, but once tragedy strikes, the face of comedy sobers up fast enough. What can reverse expectation, shattering illusion, so firmly and utterly? It may seem like begging the question to say that the unthinkable has happened. And yet it is important to notice that what we normally expect is what we can understand, what we understand being a future so open that we do not have to live constantly with the fear that it will stop. Tragedy stops everything. Before tragedy there was another world; after tragedy, who knows what? Even though Oedipus had been warned that he might kill his father and marry his mother, even though he tried to run away from his fate, the final discovery seemed incredible, unthinkable. The President of the United States is assassinated; we know it has happened, but we keep saying, "It can't really have happened." The reversal is not only too sudden to be taken in, it is the nature of such a reversal that it cannot be accepted. Even later, when we think we have got used to the tragic event, there are moments when, without warning, we are overwhelmed by the

41

full force of the reversal, as fresh almost as the first time. So we feel about the death of persons we love.

We would not feel like this if their death were temporary, like their leaving for a trip abroad. It is the irreversibility of tragedy that makes it so unthinkable. Tragedy is indelible loss and waste. Man is brought in tragedy to a place where he would rather not be and from which he cannot emerge unscathed. To one who receives the full impact of significant loss and waste, life will never be the same again. Neither accustomed tasks nor comic release will ever completely erase the knowledge gained from such a thorough reversal of illusion and expectation. Not only has virtue or life been destroyed; confidence in life itself has been broken. Life cannot be depended on to cooperate in not upsetting plans and constructed securities. Life, in short, has a different character from wishes. It is odd that something so obvious as this should not be accepted by us. There is a chasm, however, between accepting something intellectually and accepting something emotionally. Joseph Conrad once said, "No human being could bear a steady view of moral solitude without going mad."[3] Similarly, no human being can bear a steady view of tragedy without going mad. Each person, no doubt, has his own limit of tolerance. Each man has, often without his knowing it, a view of the world which when shattered will leave him paralyzed, in bewilderment as well as in grief.

The world revealed by tragedy is one of "problems" that one can do nothing about. It may be a world in which one becomes aware of reality as mysterious for the first time. But it still is a world of specific events and situations, suddenly disclosed as problematic and questionable. For there can be

[3] *Under Western Eyes* (New York: New Directions, 1951), p. 39.

problems which cannot be solved, and questions that cannot be answered, however reluctant we may be to admit it. Indeed, it is precisely the person who goes on believing that all problems can be solved and all questions answered, who falls into the trap set by the reversals of tragic suffering.

Tragic suffering is unassimilable suffering for which there has been or can be no preparation. It is quite proper, therefore, to use the image of the "trap," or the room with no exit, or the prison cell in death row. The point that binds these well-worn images together is the concept of finality. Man moves through life toward death, "a being-unto-death," passing beyond limited goals or ends along the way, living within limits which he becomes acquainted with by trial and error. None of these limits, even the ultimate one, his extinction, prevents the normal person from functioning and moving on. Death is a concept relating to an indefinite future, as if it were someone else's future, not his own. The world around him, especially those parts that he has come to care about, has become a fixture to be counted on. When this world, or some significant portion of it, fails, the whole world symbolically fails too. That brings the spiritual life to what Father William F. Lynch has called "the very last point of human finitude and helplessness."[4]

To be made to feel so helpless that one does not see why he should make an effort to go on is humiliating. But the bitterness that brings forth the cynicism of Gloucester in *King Lear* ("As flies to wanton boys are we to th' gods; they kill us for their sport"[5]) represents a type of helplessness that itself is not final. As long as you can explain tragedy by ascribing it to anything so simple as an opposition between "us" and fate,

[4] *Christ and Apollo* (New York: Sheed and Ward, 1960), p. 66.

[5] Act IV, scene i, lines 36–37.

43

you have not experienced the worst. "The worst is not so long as we can say 'This is the worst' " (Edgar in *King Lear*).[6] No, the worst is when you are too overwhelmed by the reversal of the expected and accepted order to offer philosophical explanations. It is safer to speak, with James Joyce, of a "secret cause." To tell the truth, so long as you can speak at all you are but a spectator. Henry Adams, trying to share a lesson from his own grief, with a friend who needed consoling, wrote of "my own formula that I always expect the worst, and always find it worse than I expected."[7] That is what tragedy is like. You cannot anticipate the difference it will make. As Virginia Woolf put it, "One moment free; the next this."[8] "We live without a future. That's what's queer: with our noses pressed to a closed door."[9]

At the ultimate point of human finitude there seems to be no justice. Neither virtue nor innocence guarantees immunity against victimization. "He destroyeth the perfect and the wicked."[10] Job's answer to his friend Eliphaz' unfeeling question, "Who ever perished being innocent?"[11] was in effect, "Lots of people and all the time." Nevertheless, Job could also say, "Though he slay me, yet will I trust him."[12] He could trust God even in God's silence. And it is hard to think of God's speech out of the whirlwind as a relevant answer to Job. Jung was right when he suggested that "Yahweh must become man precisely because he has done man a wrong."[13] God ignored

[6] Act IV, scene i, lines 28–29.
[7] *Letters of Henry Adams*, September 5, 1909, to Henry Cabot Lodge.
[8] *A Writer's Diary*, p. 207.
[9] *Ibid.*, p. 364.
[10] Job 9:22.
[11] *Ibid.*, 4:7.
[12] *Ibid.*, 13:15.
[13] *Answer to Job* (London: Routledge, 1954).

Job's questions the way self-righteous guilt sometimes ignores embarrassing questions, by trying to make Job feel small. A callous or arrogant God, despite his whirlwind, does not even attempt to answer Job's questions, and expects him to be pleased to receive new sons and daughters to replace the old ones. Better to have been given a new wife to replace the old scolding one.

This may be the kind of situation that Lucien Goldmann had in mind when he said, "That God should be always absent and always present is the real center of the tragic vision."[14] And it may cover Job's situation, but it does not cover the more complete solitude of tragic man. It only applies to someone who has believed or still does in part believe in God. This is the reason why it is safer to think of tragic reversal as simply the reversal from what we take for granted, not as a reversal of an order of things watched over by God. It is not by any means necessary to bring in God in order to express the darkest disillusion of the human spirit. Indeed, life is even darker if there is no point outside tragedy to refer the reversal to.

If it is tragic for man to believe in God and then find God unresponsive to suffering, it is more tragic to suffer without even the memory of belief. Perhaps Goldmann's view of tragedy is not radical enough. When he says, "If there were a single human being in the world who could understand the words of tragic man and reply to them, then there would be a possible human community in the world,"[15] he forgets that there are many human beings who do understand tragic words,

---

[14] *The Hidden God* (New York: The Humanities Press, 1964), p. 37; see also Leslie Dewart's *The Future of Belief* (New York: Herder and Herder, 1966), pp. 122–25.

[15] *The Hidden God*, p. 69.

just because they live in the shadow of tragedy. There has always been a community of sufferers, rather, many communities, and I do not mean theatrical audiences. This does not mean that because they understand they can also explain or justify. Their understanding would be superficial and beside the point if they tried to. But they can hold on to each other, and that is a great deal. It is those who have no one—man, woman, or God—to hold on to, or think they do not, who suffer most. Theirs is a terrible solitude.

Having reached this self-enclosure they may give up, like Jocasta in *King Oedipus*. They cannot assimilate the unthinkable. They may, like most people, in time find their way back to routines and illusions, finally able to say piously, "Well, it could have been worse, you know." Or, they may cry, "Help me, help me." And in time, if help comes, whether from God or man, they may come to feel that in some strange way all was not lost. We may ask, at any stage of escape or progress, "What price life; is life worth the disappearance of persons, the maiming, the torture, the insults, the deprivations?" Only those who suffer have a right to answer us. At least, nobody else has a right to answer them.

Tragedy Is Not Dead

Perhaps we are wrong in assuming that no one is immune to tragedy. Such a point of view runs counter to the well-known argument that tragedy is dead. Articulated for the first time in 1929 by Joseph Wood Krutch,[16] and more recently elaborated by George Steiner,[17] its plausibility has rested largely on its assumption of the decline of moral idealism and Christian

[16] "The Tragic Fallacy," *The Modern Temper* (New York: Harcourt, Brace, and World, 1956).

[17] *The Death of Tragedy* (New York: Alfred A. Knopf, 1961).

belief. Its advocates have had to ignore a widespread interest in tragedy in the past twenty years, an interest that is not confined to academic circles. When John F. Kennedy was shot, it should have been apparent to anyone that the tragic sense of life was still as alive and valid as in the days of Sophocles and Shakespeare. Obviously Mr. Krutch and his successors were mistaken.

The issue is important, far more important than a tired academic argument. The issue is whether mankind in certain places and at certain times can experience catastrophe without caring. In order to answer affirmatively, it is not enough to point to a decline in religious belief or moral idealism; it would be necessary to assume that some people, or some societies, can live without feeling either sympathy or admiration. Such people would not be moved by the disappearance of persons or by any significant reversal in anyone's life. Unquestionably, everyone will not be moved by the same events and persons. Unquestionably, some human beings seem incapable of caring for anyone but themselves, and look on the sufferings of others without feeling. When we call them "inhuman" we are only attesting to an ideal of humanity of our own, without resolving the question of the universality of sympathy and admiration. Perhaps it is not yet necessary to try to discuss this question directly anyway. For there is not enough evidence available that the majority of mankind at any time have been so devoid of a capacity for sympathy and admiration that they cannot be moved by the downfall of someone somewhere. The almost universal grief—in all parts of the world—after John F. Kennedy's assassination should have shown once for all that the announcements of tragedy's death were premature.

This does not mean that there are not always individuals who are so unfeeling, or so full of hate, that there are no bonds

47

between them and others. Nor does it mean that some men, even many men, cannot be turned into "appendages to a machine" (Marx). If they could speak, they might say, with Rinaldi in *Farewell to Arms*, "I don't think, I operate." Nor does it mean that society cannot indoctrinate, brainwash, make men in such an image. It can and for a time it does. Possibly in the future it can be invariably successful. We cannot tell about that. At present we have other perils to worry about—above all, the trivializing of our values, attitudes, and actions. It takes something as large as the assassination of a president—and a particular kind of president at that—to revivify a stunted sense of a scale of values. The word "tragedy," like the word "divine," has been used so indiscriminately that it has become almost meaningless. And one has good reason to suspect that many people no longer feel the need to differentiate between one kind of loss and another, or of one kind of good and another.

This failure to discriminate in understanding, feeling, and language arises from more than one cause. No doubt of it, we live in a time when moral and religious commitments are shaky, to say the least. It is hard to discriminate if you are not sure of your values. But there is another reason as well, a very powerful one at that, namely, the universal dependence on a belief in an open future. As long as a person takes his future for granted, and the ambience, physical and cultural, that he is used to, he will be protected against radical doubt and emotional panic. The same dependence, the stronger it is—and in a time of weakening of old values, it will be very strong indeed—will be especially vulnerable to some exceptional reversal. And so the tragic sense of life, apparently dead, will revive with all its old power to move and to instruct.

A tragic sense of life does not depend on the individual. No one wants tragedy for himself, however much he likes looking at someone else's. There is, therefore, some truth in Joseph K.'s boasting, "It's only a trial if I recognize it as such." A reversal of fortune is tragic only if we are able to recognize it, and tragic for others as well only if we have learned to distinguish between kinds of reversal. In short, there are reversals that are intrinsically trivial and reversals that are intrinsically important. It is helpful to use different terms to refer to them, or at the very least to think of them as different kinds of tragedy. Perhaps we should do both.

It is easy to see a difference between the fall of a strong man and the fall of a weak one, between a highly reflective man and one with little insight into himself. It is easy to see a difference between the death of someone with promise or someone who has known success, and someone who has achieved little or nothing and has only shoddy dreams of glory. We may find it in ourselves to pity the latter as well as the former, but we would do well to find out whether our sympathies arise from admiration, genuine fellow feeling, or from condescension. Between high tragedy and pathos there is space for many kinds of reversal of fortune and much sympathy, even a high degree of poignancy on behalf of some who are not themselves great but who, but for mistaken judgment, might have been. This is what Lukàcs meant when he said that "in order to enter the universe of tragedy, men must reach a very high threshold of perfection."[18] The higher the perfection the more irrational and more challenging is the reversal. It is easier to remain unmoved by the death of Arthur Miller's Willy Loman than

[18] *The Hidden God,* p. 49.

the torments of Job and Oedipus. Weakness has less claim to attention or survival; wisdom and responsibility have much more. The nature of the cause of suffering is directly related to the character of the person affected. If the cause is hidden, it is because one cannot explain how or why a good person is destroyed. One does not worry about fools and knaves.

Just as there are gradations of tragic sympathy, tragic causation, and tragic heroism, so there are different sorts of serious tragedy as well. There is the tragedy of the fallen hero (Achilles) and the trial of the innocent (Job). There is a tragedy in excusable ignorance (Oedipus) and a tragedy of promise (Patroclus). There can be a tragedy of flawed nobility (Lear) and a tragedy of the absurd (Kafka). There are often in the twentieth century conflicts between loyalties, conflicts between desire and commitment, between commitment and commitment, between the concrete and the abstract, the old and the new, the secular and the divine. The types are as many and as varied as the situations in which men can be overturned. Karl Jaspers is mistaken in supposing that "tragedy becomes the privilege of the exalted few."[19] It is open to everyone, to experience both first-hand and vicariously. It is not open to everyone to appreciate every kind of tragic reversal, or even to experience every kind.

All men die, and most see others die—two different kinds of experience right there—and death fits the canons of tragedy as neatly as any other catastrophe, except for the arbitrary distinction between the natural and the exceptional. The fact that "misfortune, suffering, and destruction from death and from evil" are "simply the burden that all must bear,"[20] does not

[19] *Tragedy Is Not Enough* (Boston: The Beacon Press, 1952), p. 99.
[20] *Ibid.*, pp. 98–99.

make them any less tragic, unless we assume arbitrarily that "there is no tragedy without transcendence,"[21] and no transcendence experienced in death. Why must we assume this? The same argument was used by Mr. Krutch to proclaim the death of all tragedy. He had said that "every real tragedy is an affirmation of faith in life," "triumph over despair,"[22] and he assumed that such an affirmation or triumph was no longer possible. Not only is it possible, it is possible even before death. One need not, however, go so far as this. Whether such an affirmation is the sign of illusion or the mark of some deep truth, whether it is a "tragic fallacy" or a tragic truth, the profound awe that accompanies tragic loss can be felt even without any affirmation whatsoever. Tragedy is no more dependent on affirmation, which in a sense cancels out the experience itself, than it is dependent on the tragic sufferer being a virtuous man with a flaw in his character.

To demand "affirmation" and "triumph" of tragic suffering is to reveal the strong temptation to speak of tragedy from the point of view of the theater-goer. For two thousand years scholars have been misled by Aristotle. To distinguish so sharply between the "natural" and the "exceptional" is to perpetuate his bias. That death comes to all is no reason for insisting that death is not in itself tragic. Simone de Beauvoir, recalling her mother's hard death, has said: "There is no such thing as a natural death: nothing that happens to a man is ever natural, since his presence calls the world into question. All men must die: but for every man his death is an accident and, even if he knows it and consents to it, an unjustifiable violation."[23] This last phrase aptly sums up the tragic sense. Thus

[21] *Ibid.*, p. 41.
[22] "The Tragic Fallacy," pp. 84–86.
[23] *A Very Easy Death* (New York: G. P. Putnam's Sons, 1966), p. 106.

the critical distinction between natural or accidental, and exceptional or meaningful, becomes arbitrary and irrelevant.

Spectator Versus Sufferer

Theories of tragedy are almost always concerned with either literature or theater, and therefore they are preoccupied with the point of view of the spectator, what he sees and how he responds. In the first place, what is presented and talked about is imitation, not real suffering; in the second place, the concern of the writer is that of a spectator and a critic, not that of a fellow sufferer, and above all not that of someone talking about himself. Perhaps it has been assumed that the lessons of artistic tragedy are the same, only privileged, as those of real-life tragedy. But such an assumption, if anyone bothered to think of it, would be misleading. Man learns certain lessons from being involved in life, and certain others from looking on life and fiction. However powerful a representation of life may be, it is still only a representation, and the emotional response it evokes, however sympathetic, will nonetheless be easier to put out of mind than that evoked by the suffering of the person one cares most for in real life. In a sense, the spectator's pity and terror come cheap and are easily purged. To tell the truth, there is nothing more natural than to expect catharsis to take place fairly quickly. Once the book is closed or the stage emptied, there is no lingering evidence of catastrophe to keep the emotions of pity and terror at pitch. The problem for the author or playwright is not whether he can effect a catharsis, but what kind. Will pity and terror be replaced by affirmative feelings or by distaste?

Aristotle did not attempt to conceal his point of view, that of the critical spectator of theatrical tragedy. His examples were taken from the theater, and his major interest lay in his

52

attempt to define the kind of character who could evoke certain emotional responses from the audience. No wonder that he not only did not grapple with the problem of causation—except by referring without discussion to an assumed "flaw" in the tragic hero—but avoided the fundamental element of fate and the irrational always present in the kind of reversal of fortune that he was writing about. One result of his bias was that he had to do violence to Sophocles' representation of the innocence of Oedipus in order to avoid recognizing the element of the irrational in Oedipus' downfall.

There is no point blaming Aristotle for what followed. But it is time to consider the lessons of real-life tragedy and stop assuming that they are the same as the lessons of theatrical tragedy. Even Nietzsche, as independent as he was, could not shake this bias completely. But with Nietzsche a new start was made. He understood something, even from his reading, of "the terrors and horrors of existence," "the nausea," "the panic," "the ecstasy," "the absurdity."[24] What a difference from Aristotle! And he could explain why existence sometimes, in tragedy, seems absurd and evokes awe, "the tremendous awe which seizes man when he suddenly begins to doubt the cognitive modes of experience, in other words, when in a given instance the law of causation seems to suspend itself."[25] It is when a reversal of fortune forces men to see the world they had formerly taken for granted as meaningless or illusory, that they feel panic and awe. And those who are, even from a distance and vicariously, "united with the secret cause" (Joyce), can also in compassion be united with other people in their suffering.

Nietzsche, who wrote *The Birth of Tragedy* when he was a

[24] *The Birth of Tragedy* (New York: Anchor Books, 1956).
[25] *Ibid.*, p. 22.

53

young man, understood the category of suffering from the inside. And yet the artist, the critic, the spectator won out in the end. Even with "the hero destroyed," he optimistically wrote of being lifted "above the whirl of shifting phenomena."[26] The spectator's perspective had blurred the subjectivity of suffering. As elsewhere in Nietzsche's writings the pages are sprinkled with the holy water of euphoria. We must say this because we know something of the poignant gap between his private heartache and his philosophical rhetoric. If ever there was a man who tried to convince himself that black is white, it was Nietzsche. The man who himself was unacquainted with solace, wrote with such absolute assurance of the "metaphysical solace" to be found in tragedy. Whose tragedy? We can only assume that he meant theatrical tragedy, someone else's suffering.

What sleight of hand could transform terror into acceptance? The answer is that Nietzsche's critical perspective was not consistent. He began by thinking of real suffering; he ended by thinking of theatrical suffering. He was quite right in calling the spectator's final response to tragedy "metaphysical solace," although he did not define this solace consistently. Indeed, he has left us two definitions, an early one and a late one. In *The Birth of Tragedy* he said that "for a moment we become the primal Being,"[27] reality "not in the phenomena but behind them."[28] By the time he wrote *Ecce Homo*, at the end of his sanity, he had developed an intense antipathy toward metaphysics and its categories. He could no longer believe in the validity of a distinction between phenomena and anything "behind," "above," or "beneath" them. By that time he was

[26] *Ibid.*, p. 102.
[27] *Ibid.*
[28] *Ibid.*

sure reality is nothing but phenomena, flux, "becoming." He had come to reject tragic catharsis, arguing that a man should "not relieve himself of terror and pity . . . but rather far beyond . . . to be the eternal joy of becoming itself."[29] In other words, Nietzsche wanted to persuade himself that the initial terror in the face of absurdity is an emotional mistake, a mistake in judgment. Tragedy should inspire joy rather than terror. Easier said than done. And, in any event, it is easier to say this in the face of theatrical suffering than in face of real suffering.

Nietzsche would have been more convincing had he shown some reluctance to go beyond the facts, and had he, like our contemporary Murray Krieger, spoken of "the unresolvable tension that must now replace tragedy's more sublime catharsis as its principle of aesthetic control."[30] And yet even Mr. Krieger betrays his spectator's bias, in mentioning "aesthetic control." Whether one can or cannot accept unresolvable tension, the attempt to do so shows an intention to remain faithful to the initial impact and truth of tragic reversal. It is this fidelity which is always betrayed by those who, again from a spectator's point of view, talk of catharsis. Father William Lynch's impressive discussion of tragedy, as sensitive as Krieger's to the tension, the absurdity, the helplessness, is misleading at this point. "In tragedy the spectator is brought to the experience of a deep beauty and exaltation, but not by the way of beauty and exaltation."[31] The question is not whether one can learn to accept tragedy, but whether, far beyond that, one

[29] *Ecce Homo*, in *The Philosophy of Nietzsche* (New York: Modern Library, 1927), p. 868.

[30] "Tragedy and the Tragic Vision," *Tragedy: Modern Essays in Criticism*, ed. Laurence Michel and Richard B. Sewall (Englewood Cliffs, N.J.: Prentice-Hall, 1963), p. 145.

[31] *Christ and Apollo*, p. 67.

can be exalted by it. The answer has usually been, "Yes, if the suffering is not real, or not real to you." What will the answer be if we shift our scrutiny away from the novel and the theater and turn to ourselves and those we admire or love in real life? When tragedy falls on them, we may feel awe—sometimes mistaken for exaltation—but an awe very likely followed by bitterness, numbness, or total loss of faith.

Life, Not Theater

Because tragedy is the worst that can happen to the best, the figure of Oedipus will always be a most lucid guide to help us deal with suffering. The passion of Jesus Christ and the sufferings of Job would be of equal use were it not for their endings, which are somewhat less ambiguous than that of Oedipus. Oedipus is received by Zeus in death, but unlike them he experiences neither restoration nor resurrection. Although Oedipus, like Job and Christ, had to suffer from misunderstanding and rejection, Oedipus had the additional distinction of having helped bring about a fate worse than death. Job and Christ had, after all, done nothing shameful, and did not have to put up with the morbid curiosity of every stranger about a fate too embarrassing to think about. It may be that mankind is by nature drawn toward evil because evil is the opposite of all man lives by; it is more likely that attraction to evil, whether in thought or deed, is a kind of evidence of our fascination with the mystery of human freedom. Dostoevsky's discussions of this in *Notes from Underground* and *The Brothers Karamazov* would seem to confirm this. Indeed, when men are no longer sure of their values, their wills sicken, and they seem drawn to evil almost for the sake of evil itself.

No one can accuse Oedipus of having a sick will. His tremendous energy and his devotion to truth are proved by his sense of responsibility for others. Had he been a weaker or more selfish man, he would not have killed his father and married his mother. This, the chief among almost countless ironies in his story, makes him the darkest of men. And this is why his story "is told everywhere and never dies."[32] It is especially tragic, the quintessence of tragedy, when a man does the very thing he disapproves of most, and without knowing it until afterwards. And this suffering is, in the case of Sophocles' representations of Oedipus in two plays (Aristotle notwithstanding), unrelieved by any reason for blaming Oedipus himself. If this is not clear after seeing or reading *Oedipus the King*, there is not the slightest excuse for doubt by the time we have finished *Oedipus at Colonus*. Again and again Oedipus protests his complete innocence, angrily and harshly. Could the indignation have been Sophocles' as well, weary of hearing people try to explain away tragedy? And at the end of the play (the end also of Sophocles' life and reflection on suffering) Oedipus the innocent is accepted on his own terms by the gods.

Oedipus underwent a course in darkness. The imagery of darkness dominates both plays. Led by Apollo, sun god, and his own dark genius, under cover of ignorance he seeks and finds the evils he has sought to escape, uncovers his hidden life and in dread recognition blinds himself. His mother and wife had warned, "May you never come to know who you are, unhappy man."[33] Translated into a universal admonition, this means, "May we never know what we may become!" Having violated nature, his presence makes humans shudder. Exiled, that others may not be reminded of the power of fate, he is led,

---

[32] *Oedipus at Colonus*, trans. Robert Fitzgerald, in *Greek Plays in Modern Translation*, ed. Dudley Fitts (New York: Dial Press, 1947), p. 406.

[33] *King Oedipus*, trans. William Butler Yeats, *ibid.*, p. 372.

once again by Apollo, to the sacred grove of "the sweet children of original darkness and earth"[34] at Colonus. A place has been reserved for him by the chthonic gods in chthonic night. At the next to the last hour both brother-in-law and son try to divert him from this destiny: only the compassion of Theseus, king of Athens, saves him. "I too was an exile. I know I am only a man; I have no more to hope for in the end than you."[35] And so Oedipus, "taught by time, suffering, and royalty in the blood,"[36] accompanied by his faithful daughters and protected by Theseus, is ready for his apotheosis.

The testimony of Sophocles is all the more to be pondered because it is so modest. He does not speak of exaltation or triumph. The last moments of Oedipus' life are somber and awesome. There is thunder offstage, the god's voice is reported but not heard by the audience. Oedipus walks off the stage, and not even Theseus or Oedipus' daughters, who walked with him into the grove, can tell the manner of his disappearance. The god had called him, "That one, that one, Oedipus, why are we waiting?"[37] Oedipus then went forward, and, despite his blindness, needed no help from those whose eyes could see. And the god received him. It was, as the survivors assure each other—as they like to do—an end without pain. If Apollo had misled Oedipus, Zeus redeemed him. Carl Jung, rephrasing Christian theology, had said of Job that God did him a wrong and became man to make up for it. But Sophocles could not imagine a redemption for Oedipus any more adequate or any less. We should try to respect his integrity.

[34] *Oedipus at Colonus*, p. 391.

[35] *Ibid.*, p. 408.

[36] *Oedipus at Colonus* (Greek text), in *Sophoclis Fabulae*, ed. A. C. Pearson (London: Oxford University Press, 1964), lines 7–8.

[37] *Ibid.*, line 1627.

What he was concerned about in this legend was the irrational. "All we have seen and suffered is irrational."[38] And he offered two kinds of encouragement to those who descend into the special darkness of the irrational. Antigone recollected that Oedipus' last words had been of love, "One word, love, loosens burdens."[39] He had received that from her and Ismene. In the symbolic acceptance by Zeus it is as if Sophocles were saying, "I cannot prove this, but no one can suffer as gratuitously as Oedipus and not be blessed in some way." Athens, his burial place, will benefit. He himself would have his belief in his innocence confirmed. The chorus carries Sophocles' last words, "Stop weeping, these things have authority."[40] They certainly do, if emotional response to theater is any guide. But we may suppose that Sophocles, like any serious writer, was not concerned only, or mainly, with theater, but through theater with life itself. His testimony, therefore, is evidence of the direction of his own hope, but it is not evidence independent of that hope. We are left with the problem with which we began, what to think of the unthinkable. Can a man look the irrational in the face and die—I was about to say live— happily?

[38] *Ibid.*, line 1675.
[39] *Ibid.*, line 1617.
[40] *Ibid.*, lines 1777–79.

III

The Darkness
of God

4

The Silence of God

It is when from the uttermost depths of our being we need a sound which does mean something—when we cry out for an answer and it is not granted—it is then that we touch the silence of God.—Simone Weil

Man Lost

Most unhappy states are concentrated experiences. The main difference between those who experience tragedy and despair and those who have a sense of the absence of God is that the first are centered on themselves and the second on the breakdown of their world of meaning. Moreover, these may either come to think of their fate as tragic or may sink to a depressive immobility. This does not mean that all experiences of darkness are reducible to any one form, but rather that it is possible for the human spirit to slip back and forth from one form to another, according as it is concerned with what has happened to the self or what has happened to meaning.

The revelation of God is thought of in biblical terms under two images, Light and Word. Man needs light in the darkness of his sin and finitude, and he does not have enough light of his own. But the light that can lighten every man (if he does not reject it) is the Word, Covenant and Law, the proclamation of the prophets, and the living Word of the Son of God. As long as revelation is heard, and, to some extent, obeyed, man believes in it, but as he learns through it to free his own

63

powers of understanding and making, he needs the Word less and less. This is the crisis Dietrich Bonhoeffer and others in our century have called our attention to. Man "comes of age" and no longer needs God for many of the unsolved problems on the edge of existence, for they are now soluble. And therefore God Himself and His biblical revelation seem irrelevant and unreal.

Some men march confidently toward a future of their own designing, uninterested in the old question of ultimate meaning. For their God neither speaks nor is silent, unless for reasons of their own personal history they still want the luxury of believing in a transcendent God and believing in self-sufficient selves. Only those who are troubled by the indeterminacy of this same planned future, their own fallibility, and above all are still made uneasy by death and moral conflict, those would still like to hear a Word of reassurance. And they are no longer able to hear it. For their God is somehow still desirable and yet silent. They feel themselves to be in a silent dark.

Darkness and silence always have much in common. They both protect and imprison. When voices have become unbearably insistent, silence is the ambience of dreamed-of peace. And when companionship and confirmation are needed, silence only emphasizes a person's loneliness. The more lonely we are, the more sinister the silence. This is as true on a metaphysical level as it is on an interpersonal level. Indeed, at earlier stages of civilized development than our own, the clearest mark of man's feeling of vulnerability was his natural transference of the anxieties of his psychological experience to a metaphysical plane. What he could not resolve by himself or with other persons, he tried to resolve by means of religious imagination.

Today that kind of imagination is inoperative for most and

only thinly functioning for the rest. At one time, and for many centuries, religious imagination was not only taken as real, it was absolutely impelling. The divine manifested itself not in ideas or in cinematic projection of metaphors, as in modern books on religion, but in voices and visions apparently made of the stuff of the physical world. To say that God spoke, or an angel appeared, was not just a way of establishing the credibility of a new idea, it was a literal description of some happening. Today religious symbolism is a relatively sophisticated way of retaining the aspect of mystery that accompanies personal disclosures. To a more primitive mind, as to a psychologically unbalanced one, divine revelation was received with the same mixture of surprise and acceptance as any other interpersonal encounter. To say so much is not to claim any inside knowledge of primitive experience, but simply to indicate the unbridgeable chasm between one kind of psychological experience and another.

Few now claim to hear God speak, and they are for the most part in mental institutions. For all their claims to infallibility, popes seem to have been even less blessed with concrete manifestations of the divine than many of their saintlier subjects. It is also noteworthy that God Himself has not addressed man directly and with the same frequency in recent centuries as during the ages of the Jewish patriarchs and prophets. On the other hand, He may have delegated this function to some of the saints, particularly the Blessed Virgin Mary. Ours is a disbelieving age, and even when otherwise honest men and women recount to us their dreams and visions we do not readily believe them, and their experiences fade into the limbo of hallucinations and premonitions.

One thing has not changed across the ages: man's hunger for certainty. Whether he has achieved it or lost it, that may change, but the need and quest for certainty has remained. He cannot get along without some measure of it. Since most men live off the certainties and uncertainties of more powerful men than they, it is fruitless to wonder whether sophisticated witnesses were representative of their times or exceptions thrown up on the shore. It does not matter, for example, whether Pascal was a spokesman for a cultural crisis in the seventeenth century or a spiritual contemporary of our own. His language is partly our own and partly the common biblical inheritance. For him God was not silent so much as hidden. ("Truly, you are a hidden God" Isaiah 45:15.) But when Pascal spoke of man as lost in a silent universe, he was saying something slightly new, even though in the end it comes to the same thing.

Pascal has little to tell us of God, indeed somewhat less than we would know if we had read the Bible as carefully as Karl Barth. But he had something to say about man that still seems fresh. When he writes of the intellectual fallibility of man, his skepticism is no more original, and no more profound, than that of many another philosopher of the past two centuries. In fact, his numerous references to Montaigne show that he was obsessed with the skepticism of his age. What distinguished him so completely from Montaigne and from our own contemporary skepticism was Pascal's intense uneasiness over human fallibility. It exists, but would that it did not. Man is "incapable of certain knowledge and of absolute ignorance";[1] "nothing shows him the truth, everything deceives him."[2] And that is a terrible state to be in, albeit it is "the condition of man." Pascal cannot emotionally accept the insecurity of the human condition: "I look on all sides and see only darkness every-

[1] Pascal, *Pensées*, par. 72.
[2] *Ibid.*, par. 83.

where . . . nothing which is not a matter of doubt and concern
. . . seeing too much to deny and too little to be sure . . .
ignorant of what I am or of what I ought to do, I know neither
my condition nor my duty."[3]

It is his constant use of the image of "darkness" that is the
measure of the difference between his skepticism and Montaigne's. For his own uncertainty about man becomes almost
total in his admission that (without Jesus Christ) we are
incapable of knowing either what God is or if He is. He never
quite advocated St. Augustine's notion that a man can find
himself only by finding God, although like Augustine he was
convinced that he had too little knowledge of God to be able to
know himself. Uncertainty is never total as long as there is any
nostalgia. It is only when man no longer feels nostalgic, when
his spirit has become numb, that his uncertainty is really total.
Pascal makes use of several metaphors to express the depth of
his disillusionment. Each image serves also to remind us of
what we are missing. "Nothing stays for us."[4] And yet we have
a "secret instinct, a remnant of the greatness of our original
nature, which teaches us that happiness consists only in rest."[5]
Is this why the condition of man is "inconstancy, boredom,
restlessness"?[6] He changes the image only slightly when he
says that "we sail within a vast sphere, ever drifting in uncertainty."[7] To be in motion when we deeply need rest is bad, but
to move directionless and without motive is worse.

Certainty depends on a fixed point of reference beyond the
needs of the self. It seems unnecessary to have to justify the

[3] *Ibid.*, par. 229.
[4] *Ibid.*, par. 72.
[5] *Ibid.*, par. 139.
[6] *Ibid.*, par. 127.
[7] *Ibid.*, par. 72.

need for certainty. It is one of the absolutes of human nature, all the more insistent when it is lacking. If to stand is good, there must first be something firm to stand on. Similarly, if to be certain is good, no certainty can be expected as long as we take practically nothing for granted. That is the way Pascal feels when he says, "Our whole groundwork cracks, and the earth opens to abysses."[8] There is little emotional difference between this metaphor and physiological vertigo and nausea, a space in which man discovers that he is "lost in this remote corner of nature."[9]

Pascal's famous comparison of man with the infinite, an atom in an infinity of universes, is calculated to frighten by sheer immeasurability. "The end of things and their beginning are hopelessly hidden from him in an impenetrable secret."[10] No wonder that man cannot locate himself. Today we would say, no wonder that man does not feel he belongs. Perhaps Pascal was not concerned about belonging to the cosmos, only because he still could belong to Parisian society. Our alienation is, however, more complete. One of the characteristic features of Pascal's mind is his tendency to see counterparts everywhere. Man does not know God; he does not know himself either. Man lives in darkness, and carries darkness around with him. Man is lost, but so is God.[11] Is there a bittersweet consolation in this? If I am lost, well, God is just as lost. If I have darkness inside me, that is all right, for darkness is everywhere. If I cannot know myself, well, take comfort, I do

[8] *Ibid.*

[9] *Ibid.*; Cf. Teilhard de Chardin's "Man, the center of perspective, is at the same time the center of construction of the universe" *The Phenomenon of Man* (New York: Harper and Row, 1965), p. 33.

[10] *Pensées*, par. 72.

[11] *Ibid.*, par. 441: "Nature is such that she testifies everywhere both within man and without him, to a lost God and a corrupt nature."

not know God at all. Things are pretty bad; in fact, they could not be much worse.

But Pascal was wrong; things can be worse, as we shall see. His polemical nature, his contempt for empty-heads and play-boys, his daring to wager, indicate a nervous balance that is missing from many equally skeptical minds of our own time. He could feel lost, and yet not panic. He could wander in "impenetrable darkness"[12] and yet converse with us as if in broad daylight. For he had a prime nostalgic sense of man having "fallen from his true place without being able to find it again."[13] It might seem to us now that Pascal was suffering from a metaphysical experience relatively new in his age, as again and again he speaks of "the frightful spaces of the universe which surround me."[14] So far is this from our "space age," in which space has been made familiar by camera and rocket, the fright comes from the inner experience of the beholder, not from stargazing. It is not the natural scientist in Pascal who was frightened, but a philosopher who had learned well the limitations of habit, prejudice, the deceptions of the senses, and the fallibility of logic, and who knew that he could receive no more infallible truth than he could give. If this is enlightenment, then enlightenment is a way of describing man's coming of age, shedding the romantic illusions of child-hood.

Nostalgia

It is instructive to compare Pascal's appraisal of man's metaphysical position and Camus'. The latter is less disturbed, more matter-of-fact. His was "a world where everything is

[12] *Ibid.*, par. 194.
[13] *Ibid.*, par. 427.
[14] *Ibid.*, par. 194.

given and nothing is explained."[15] And in spite of his fondness for the word "absurd" he was reluctant to call the world absurd. "The world in itself is not reasonable, that is all that can be said."[16] But Pascal had not yet had time to get used to disillusionment. Not only was man no longer the center or in the absolute center of the universe, he did not know how to explain where he was, for there were no fixed points of reference left. His reaction to this is contained in such images as "the frightful spaces" and "the whole silent universe," and above all in his many allusions to "darkness" (*ténèbres*), and his insistence on "the misery of man."

With Pascalian clarity Camus wrote of "a universe suddenly divested of illusions and lights."[17] But his feeling about this is different. "Man feels an alien, a stranger. His exile is without remedy since he is deprived of the memory of a lost home or the hope of a promised land."[18] To some there may not seem to be much difference between fright and loneliness, but the difference is considerable. The terror is in part past, and, whatever is to come, there has been time already to become reconciled to the new condition. And yet when we try to distinguish between disillusion and resignation, about all that can be usefully said is that disillusion is more unstable, and may be succeeded by a return to intense even if irrational commitment, whereas resignation can more easily resist healing altogether.

Camus' originality lies in his conception of "the absurd," the "confrontation between the human need and the unreason-

[15] *The Myth of Sisyphus*, pp. 135–36.
[16] *Ibid.*, p. 21.
[17] *Ibid.*, p. 6.
[18] *Ibid.*

able silence of the world."[19] He thought of human need as a "wild longing for clarity,"[20] "my nostalgia for unity,"[21] and defined "the unreasonable silence of the world" as "the world that disappoints."[22] God does not speak, and the world is not self-explanatory. It would be as reasonable to ask, "Why should one care?" Camus did care. His repeated use of the word "nostalgia" indicates his resignation and regret on the one hand, and his idealism on the other. His idealism was not one that could be satisfied emotionally or intellectually by an impulsive leap toward the irrational, but rather by patient explorations in a state of extreme tension, of the possibilities of creating a just world.

The Hidden God

Camus did not have a "God-nostalgia." What he wanted was clarity—which he magnificently achieved—and unity and justice, which remain for mankind to achieve. We have only to compare him to Ingmar Bergman to realize the difference. The torment of faith represented by the disillusioned crusader in *The Seventh Seal* was not part of Camus' experience. "What is going to happen to those of us who want to believe but aren't able to? . . . Why can't I kill God within me? . . . I call out to him in the dark, but no one seems to be there."[23] Bergman's sense of "God within me" is common to those in our time who have not been able to emancipate themselves completely from their religious inheritance; it is by no means, therefore, uni-

[19] *Ibid.*, p. 28.
[20] *Ibid.*, p. 21.
[21] *Ibid.*, p. 50.
[22] *Ibid.*
[23] *Four Screenplays*, p. 112.

71

versal. Not only did Camus not call out to God, he did not seem to want to believe either. It is one thing to admit that the existence of God might make things intellectually easier; it is quite another to long for Him. That is why we must remark on the odd fact that Camus continually used the word "nostalgia" in his writings. On the one hand, he had an intense nostalgia for the North African places of his youth, for beach and sun. Otherwise, the nostalgia he refers to is for logical consistency, metaphysical unity, and moral justice. No more than Nietzsche did he show any emotional interest in a divine presence that could underwrite clarity, unity, and justice. The mystical—the religious—dimension was missing in him altogether.

While Bergman locates the hidden God within man, Pascal makes no attempt to locate him at all. Where is God hidden? Pascal does not even consider the question. The reason is that he is more concerned with the cause of God's withholding himself. "God is a hidden God . . . and since the corruption of nature, He has left men in a darkness from which they can escape only through Jesus Christ, without whom all communion with God is cut off."[24] "Nature is such that she testifies everywhere, both within man and without him, to a lost God and a corrupt nature."[25] Pascal's notion of perfection and corruption is very simplistic and harsh. Man should love God alone and hate himself, for self-love and self-will obscure his vision of God and get in the way of moral perfection.

Man lives in shadows, estranged from God, who has hidden Himself from man because man is willful and self-centered. But this is an indirect way of saying something about man rather than God. God is the same and has not moved on. It is man whose concern and therefore whose vision has changed, and

[24] *Pensées*, par. 242.
[25] *Ibid.*, par. 441.

who blames God instead of himself. On the contrary, God has gone out of His way to make it possible for blind man to find his way home. God sent His son, Jesus, so that whoever would see and follow him would see and follow God. God appears openly in Jesus but only to those who sincerely seek Him, from the heart. Pascal himself had sought God sincerely and with his whole heart, and received an extraordinary confirmation of success in an experience of the night. In the night of November 23, 1654, for two hours his whole being was fired with the joy of knowing God through Jesus Christ. What he had always believed to be true, he then experienced interiorily, namely, that God is hidden only when men are blinded by self-love, and He is revealed only in the life, person, and imitation of Jesus Christ.

This is why Lucien Goldmann falsifies Pascal's position when he says that "for Pascal God always exists but never appears."[26] For Pascal God not only exists but has appeared in Jesus Christ, and the truth and power of this appearance is preserved in the Church and sacraments. Moreover, just as we know God only through Jesus Christ, so our passions abate only as we learn to imitate the humility of Jesus Christ. This is the same sequence of discovery that St. Augustine said that he had gone through before his conversion. The difference between Pascal and Augustine at this point is that for the latter self-control and self-knowledge are one and the same (a Platonic view).

Pascal could not have agreed with Goldmann that "God is nothing more than a spectator."[27] This is to interpret the metaphor "hidden God" so literally as to go beyond the image and suggest that God, in hiding, watches man, either out of

[26] *The Hidden God*, p. 37.
[27] Georg Lukàcs, quoted by Goldmann in *The Hidden God*, p. 37.

73

indifference or out of malevolence. This is refuted by Pascal's insistence that God, far from being indifferent, sent His son Jesus Christ through whom man can know God.

Goldmann's book is primarily a proclamation of the nature of tragic thought, and he makes use of Pascal to illustrate his own perspective. The result is in part a twisting of Pascal to fit him into the theory of tragedy Goldmann has borrowed from Georg Lukàcs. Lukàcs had called tragedy "a game which is watched by God. He is nothing more than a spectator, and he never intervenes, either by word or deed."[28] This may well be true, but it is not Pascal. It is a point of view located somewhere between Camus and Bergman. The former, like Goldmann, believed that man "lives constantly in hope and never in certainty," wishing for authentic values but, like Bergman, oppressed by the unrelieved silence of God. "God's voice no longer speaks directly to man."[29] This may be so, if what is meant is that there are no longer patriarchs, prophets, or mystics who have heard God's voice, but it is not so if the revelation of God in Jesus Christ and in His body the Church is taken seriously.

Torment of Faith

For Pascal faith was an option not a torment, an option founded particularly firmly on biblical prophecies and miracles. Quite apart from the incredibility of miracles to modern men, it is much harder today to accept that option without uneasiness. The returned crusader in *The Seventh Seal* is in spirit a man of our century. "Why should he hide himself in a mist of half-spoken promises and unseen miracles?"[30] There is

[28] *Ibid.*, p. 37.
[29] *Ibid.*, p. 36.
[30] Bergman, *Four Screenplays*, p. 111.

no equivalent bitterness in Pascal, whose own experience was the opposite of that behind the knight's description of his own tormented faith: "It is like loving someone who is out there in the darkness but never appears, no matter how loudly you call."[31] This is the manner of Goldmann and Lukàcs, and is similar also to Gerard Manley Hopkins' lament, "cries countless, cries like dead letters sent to dearest him that lives alas! away."[32]

The "God who is with us is the God who forsakes us,"[33] and He is the God who has left us alone to our own devices, man having "come of age." But the God who forsakes us does not seem to everyone a God worth having. There are still men who lament the absence of God, sending out their cries like Job to disturb His silence. Is it conceivable that a man might try to comfort the God who was forsaken by reminding Him that we too are going through the wringer? Yes, of course, but it is not conceivable that one will think of Him as God for very long or get much comfort in return. This is a point that the sacristan makes in Bergman's *Winter Light*.[34] He had asked his pastor to remember that the suffering on the cross cannot be compared to much physical suffering, that to be misunderstood and forsaken by one's disciples is worse, and that even worse is concluding that God has abandoned His own son, and that the son's preaching has been only a lie. How much longer will the so-called "God-hypothesis" live on even in nostalgia?

There are still people who can neither curse nor kill God, and who, in spite of their profound skepticism, call out from

[31] *Ibid.*, p. 137.

[32] *Poems and Prose of Gerard Manley Hopkins*, No. 44.

[33] Dietrich Bonhoeffer, *Letters and Papers from Prison* (New York: Macmillan Paperbacks, 1966), p. 218.

[34] Ingmar Bergman, *Une Trilogie* (Paris: Robert Laffont, 1964), p. 190.

their darkness. If they believe that God is light beyond human darkness, they can pray with the knight, "God, You who are somewhere, who must be somewhere, have mercy upon us."[35] For them it is inconceivable that human need can be so intensely experienced, and then so indifferently left unanswered and unfulfilled. God is because we need Him. The knight's squire, however, having accepted the consequences of the destructive world made by the likes of him and his knight, parodies the supplication of the knight when he says, "In the darkness where You are supposed to be, where all of us probably are . . . in the darkness You will find no one to listen to Your cries or be touched by Your sufferings. Wash Your tears and mirror Yourself in Your indifference."[36] In Christian mysticism darkness is the place where God dwells, or to put it differently, God's light is so bright it blinds like the sun on reflecting snow. But if God is as blind, or as ignorant as man, in what sense can He be called God at all?

There is one sense left: reality is basically inhuman and malevolent. At a certain point, and after some kinds of experience of evil, religious skepticism ends, and religious pathology begins. A hypothetical God, "a God-suggestion,"[37] "a God-echo,"[38] "a God-lie"[39] are entirely different from "a spider-God."[40] According to the first metaphor man is thought of as weary of ascribing good or ill to God; the last image takes evil as so overwhelming that the whole universe seems ill-disposed. In Bergman's *Through a Glass Darkly* a father and his two children have different experiences of God. For the son, God

[35] *Four Screenplays*, p. 162.
[36] *Ibid.*, p. 162.
[37] *Une Trilogie (Les Communiants)*, p. 157.
[38] *Ibid.*
[39] *Ibid.*, p. 195.
[40] *Ibid.*, p. 157.

just does not exist. For the daughter, God comes to her as a huge spider who embraces and enters her. For the father, God exists insofar as love exists anywhere in the world, and he agrees with his son's suggestion that his psychotic daughter will be surrounded by God so long as she is surrounded by their human love. It is necessary to observe that Bergman does not wish us to suppose that only the psychotic see God as an insect. The sane too can reach such a plain of despair, like Thomas, the unbelieving pastor in *Winter Light* (or like Svidrigailov in *Crime and Punishment*), who said, "We always imagine eternity as something beyond our conception, something vast, vast! But why must it be vast? Instead of all that, what if it's one little room, like a bath-house in the country, black and grimy and spiders in every corner, and that's all eternity is?"[41] The spider-God is only a metaphorical measure of the intensity of despair.

The Ambiguity of God

The classic expression of religious despair is the psalmist's cry, "Where is now thy God?"[42] And the classic answer is Nietzsche's paraphrase of Epicurus, "If there are gods, they do not care for us." With the best will in the world orthodox Christians too have had to acknowledge the infinite distance between God's supposed goodness and the actual suffering of mankind, particularly the suffering of the innocent. Dostoevsky too was obsessed by this, and wondered whether such suffering is too high a price to pay for human freedom. Besides, there are types of physical suffering that it is still incon-

---

[41] Dostoevsky, *Crime and Punishment*, trans. Constance Garnett (New York: Heritage Press, 1938), p. 261.
[42] Psalm 42.

ceivable mankind can be held responsible for. What price victimization? One has to be spiritually complacent and callous to believe that everyone who suffers, suffers only because someone else has been careless. The more one thinks about man's inhumanity as well as the natural disasters, the more absurd and cruel to say, "Too bad, but if you want to be free and not automata, you've got to pay the price." It is when we look at the real people who do pay the price, that the irrelevance of this dawns. Cardinal Newman too believed in God, but he had to admit that "the world seems simply to give the lie to that great truth, of which my whole being is so full. . . . If I looked into a mirror and did not see my face, I should have the sort of feeling which actually comes upon me, when I look into this living busy world, and see no reflexion of its Creator."[43] The rest of this passage from his *Apologia* only would deepen our sense of loss.

There is always something worse. So here: it is bad enough to compare the truth of the heart with the truth about the world. It is much worse to have the truth about the world erase the truth of the heart. This is what happens again and again in "ordinary" life when extra-ordinary love is shattered by death, so that where there were two in one living whole, there is now only a fragmented and quivering wounded one left over. C. S. Lewis, who had been "surprised by joy" at his conversion, was equally surprised by grief when his wife died. His "observations" are part of the long record of human suffering. "Meanwhile where is God? . . . Go to him when your need is desperate . . . and what do you find? A door slammed in your face, and a sound of bolting and double bolting on the inside. After that silence. You may as well turn away. The longer you

---

[43] *Apologia pro Vita Sua* (New York: E. P. Dutton, 1946), p. 217.

wait, the more emphatic the silence will become. There are no lights in the windows. It might be an empty house. Was it ever inhabited?"[44] Just so, was it ever inhabited? Is there God at all?

Consolations do not console, for they are general and grief is specific. Besides, the consolations of religion do not really address themselves to the two great questions forced out into the open by such a loss, the final disappearance of someone loved. First, "what reason have we, except our own desperate wishes, to believe that God is, by any standard we can conceive 'good'? Doesn't all the prima facie evidence suggest exactly the opposite? . . . If God's goodness is inconsistent with hurting us, then either God is not good or there is no God; for in the only life we know He hurts us beyond our worst fears and beyond all we can imagine."[45] This divorce between what God represents and what He permits is too irrational, too absurd, for human reason and affection to assimilate. What makes the divorce harder in the case of someone like C. S. Lewis is that, unlike Ivan Karamazov, he was compelled to question the goodness of God because his own life had been shattered by the removal of a person whose love was even more real to him than God. Believing in God before he married, he could believe in God all the more after his gift of love in marriage. "Oh God, God, why did you take such trouble to force this creature out of its shell, if it is now doomed to crawl back—to be sucked back—into it?"[46] Love that is thwarted, snubbed, refused is almost as hard to bear as love betrayed; both injure pride and arrest the growth of the finest flower of human experience, self-giving. But harder still

[44] *A Grief Observed*, p. 9.
[45] *Ibid.*, p. 26.
[46] *Ibid.*, p. 18.

is the withdrawal of love once it has been fully and mutually experienced. Nothing is more disillusioning than the taking back of such a gift.

The mind has three alternatives. It can go on believing in the goodness of God. C. S. Lewis finally was able to do just this. It can convert its power to love into a powerful hatred of God, or reality in general. It can put God out of mind altogether. Men make an image of God out of their fears, but also out of love. When love is withdrawn, God may not survive even the fear of being alone. But fear may be so strong that it can invent God. So argues Alain Robbe-Grillet: "Let us retrace the functioning of solitude. I call out. No one answers me. Instead of concluding that there is no one there—which could be a pure and simple observation, dated and localized in space and time—I decide to act as if there were someone there, but someone who, for one reason or another, will not answer. The silence which follows my outcry, is henceforth no longer a true silence; it is charged with a content, a meaning, a depth, a soul."[47] The more silent God is, the more charged is the world with His presence. The evidence for this is hardly impressive, in fact there is no evidence at all, but it is a measure of the terror of the lonely heart that it can so twist the mind.

This may remind someone of the complementary parables of John Wisdom and B. G. Mitchell. Mr. Wisdom's is a tale about two explorers in a jungle who came upon a clearing. One man claimed that the flowers and weeds they found were evidence of the care of a gardener. The other disagreed. Neither could prove his claim. The skeptic finally asked the believer, "Just how does what you call an invisible, intangible, eternally elusive gardener differ from an imaginary gardener or even

[47] *For a New Novel* (New York: Grove Press, 1965), p. 3.

from no gardener at all?"[48] The result is a stand-off; it would seem to make no difference whether one believed or disbelieved in a gardener. The only question implied—and it goes un-answered in the parable—is whether there is any incontrovert-ible evidence for the existence of God.

Mr. Mitchell's story on the other hand is concerned with the mystery of evil rather than the reality of God.[49] It is told of a partisan in an occupied country who met a stranger who impressed him so much that he trusted him completely. Some-times the stranger helped him and his friends. Then the parti-san said, "He is on our side." Sometimes the stranger ap-peared in the uniform of the other side and took his friends away. Still the partisan said, "He is on our side." Finally in anger and exasperation the partisan's remaining friends said, "Well, if that's what you mean by his being on our side, the sooner he goes over to the other side the better."[50] The poig-nancy of the parable arises from its closeness to religious experience, not just religious speculation. And it is not easily relieved by talk of prophecies and miracles, by affirmations of the resurrection of Christ, or by hope of a mystical experience in the late hours of the night. The ambiguous behavior of anyone we admire is harder to take than his silence or absence.

[48] "Gods," *Logic and Language,* ed. Antony Flew (New York: Anchor Books, 1965), pp. 200–01.

[49] B. G. Mitchell, *New Essays in Philosophical Theology,* ed. A. G. N. Flew and Alasdair MacIntyre (New York: Macmillan, 1955), p. 103.

[50] *Ibid.*

5

The Dark Night

I said to my soul, be still, and let the dark come upon you
Which shall be the darkness of God.—T. S. Eliot

The Secret Silence

I believe that for the vast majority of people in the twentieth
century, including most church-goers, God is for all practical
and emotional purposes both irrelevant and unreal. And it is
hard to imagine that the average person ever thinks of God
from one Sunday to another. Everyone participates in the
silence of God, and a few experience this silence (call it
absence, lostness, death, eclipse, withdrawal) both in despera-
tion and in nostalgia. There is no logic except that of wishful
thinking which leads surely from nostalgia to hope, to say
nothing of faith. But it can be said that a human being is more
open, and by definition more human, if he is capable of
nostalgia, than if he is not. There does take place, even in
some who do not profess daily their fidelity to God, a movement from the sense of divine absence to a nostalgia for some
presence worth adoring that sets them apart from the many
who do not care at all.

In the past—and, for all we know now, for hidden souls—
another movement was often observed in those whose commitment to God was both whole-hearted and professional, a movement from a sense of God's reality and comfort to a bitter

sense of His withdrawal. In Western Christendom this has been called "the dark night of the soul." Eastern monasticism, however, while emphasizing that God is always in a darkness of incomprehensibility, seems not to have known the special bitterness of withdrawal. Perhaps Eastern Christians never allowed themselves to forget the qualitative difference between God and man, and therefore had no superficial experience of God to be exposed for the pretense that it is. Whatever the reason for the difference, it is significant, and particularly at the present time when frenzied efforts are being made to "dehellenize" the Western concept of God. It is ironic that the Hellenes do not need to dehellenize themselves.

It may seem to be a waste of time to dwell any longer on the mechanism of the dark night of the soul. In an age when even monks are turning from contemplation to action, or at least to the encouragement of action and reform, it might seem irrelevant, except for one thing. Even in the deformation of prayer symbolized by the dark night, man may seem to be escaping from God, whereas in fact he is existing all the more securely in God's love. Or, to put it differently, compared to the movement from despair to nostalgia, the dark night represents a more complex ecstatic movement from conventional faith to numbness and then to an increase of faith that should be described as lasting joy.

In any event, the oldest tradition of man's use of the image of darkness is religious. For Western man this means the biblical tradition, and of all the ways of thinking about darkness it alone is hopeful. It has its negative aspect, otherwise the image would not be used at all. But it is positive too. Mystical darkness is terrible; it is also luminous. It is full of terror because God's light is so strong, so intense, that it momentarily blinds, as the glare of sun on new fallen snow. But in the subsequent deprivation and ignorance the heat of this strange luminosity welds the soul to God.

From beginning to end the Bible makes use of images of light and darkness. Darkness signifies ignorance, and also sin and bondage. Light signifies comprehension, and also obedience and freedom. What is at stake is belief in God. If all knowledge of God is impossible, fideism notwithstanding, the credibility of belief collapses. How can man believe in that which he does not experience, and how can he experience without some sort of awareness? Without awareness of God he will be alienated, in mind, heart, behavior. Because God is such that the question of His Reality and presence is completely different from the question of the reality of the creation, the human experiencing of the darkness of God is absolutely crucial. To some it will mean getting along without even the memory of God; to others it will mean having to find some way of salvaging man's relationship with God and the integrity of the intellect.

Apart from the contemporary preoccupation with the unreality of God, there have been three major attempts to explore the darkness of God: that of Dionysius the Areopagite and Gregory of Nyssa, the English mystical tradition as represented by *The Cloud of Unknowing*, and St. John of the Cross. All three are exercises in what Dionysius and Greek Orthodox theology call apophatic or negative theology. In cataphatic or positive theology man makes affirmations about God. God exists, He is one, good, beautiful, perfect, personal, living, eternal, and so on. The affirmations are all taken from man's knowledge of creation. Nothing said about God has not already been said, by analogy, of the creation. Theologians have always acknowledged that it is misleading to apply modes of attribution taken from creation to the uncreated, and yet they have always done just that. Is there a better way? Dionysius and others have said, yes, there is. They would have been astonished at the thrashing about of many of our contemporaries who appear not to know the usefulness of negative or mystical theology. Misled by centuries of dominance of scholastic theology, most of us are belatedly discovering that affirmations about God are one thing, while the reality and presence of God are something else, and that a serious dependence on the former can prevent the mind from thinking the latter. Dionysius and Gregory knew this a long time ago.

The ordinary path of knowledge is from darkness to light, from ignorance to an ever-increasing awareness and understanding. The way of faith, on the other hand, is—at a certain stage of perfection—from light to darkness. It is not wrong to speak of God as one, good, eternal. It is not wrong to ask whether God is or is not, does or does not exist (although some say it is). What we are trying to say is clear enough. We are trying, in the first place, to attribute to God the divine perfections which His creation only approximates, and, in approximating, dreams of. We are trying, in the second place, to know whether God is real or a fiction. And all the time most of us, including the theologians, know very well that whatever we say about God, we really do think of Him as "that than which nothing is greater."[1] Whether he is "the god above gods,"[2] or "the divine incognito,"[3] we take it for granted that He is essentially nameless because He is essentially incomprehensible. Should we then keep quiet and never mention Him? Or,

[1] St. Anselm, *Proslogion, or Address to God concerning His Existence.*

[2] Paul Tillich, *The Courage To Be* (New Haven: Yale University Press, 1952), p. 186.

[3] Karl Barth, *The Epistle to the Romans* (London: Oxford University Press, 1953), p. 39.

when we mention Him, should we invent new names of contemporary relevance, like "Omega-point,"[4] or "the pressure for maturity and responsibility exerted on man by an unequivocally open future"?[5] But we know that if we keep silent about anything for long enough, it is forgotten altogether. Mystical theology would then become forgotten theology. That will not do. On the one hand, we must safeguard the mystery of God, and, on the other hand, we must be able to speak of God so that the mystery itself will not fade away. The problem is exceedingly difficult. It is even more difficult for the scholarly theologian than for the adoring worshiper, who is, at best, meeting God primarily in love rather than in conceptualizations.

Man cannot comprehend God, and when he tries he experiences darkness. His mind loses even its former impression of God's reality which its affirmations, in positive theology, took for granted. The result is numbness. "Plunging into the Darkness which is above the intellect we shall find ourselves reduced not merely to brevity of speech but even to absolute dumbness both of speech and thought."[6] God is not dark; He is simply not known or seen. This is what St. John meant when he said, "In him is no darkness at all."[7] Or, in the words of Psalm 139, "The darkness is no darkness with thee, but the night is as clear as the day; the darkness and light to thee are both alike." The divine dark, or the darkness of God, is really our darkness, the human blindness occurring whenever man tries seriously to consider the nature of God.

[4] Pierre Teilhard de Chardin, *The Phenomenon of Man.*

[5] Harvey Cox, a review of Leslie Dewart's *The Future of Belief,* Herder Correspondence, September 1966.

[6] Dionysius the Areopagite, *On the Divine Names and the Mystical Theology,* trans. C. E. Holt (London: SPCK, 1957), p. 198.

[7] I John 1:5.

If God cannot be comprehended, it is for two reasons. First, God is "that One which is beyond all things."[8] He is incomparable, and man can only know God by comparison with himself and things like him. Second, the reality of God is so overpowering that it actually prevents comprehension. God is not only different from man, He is too great for man. This is why Dionysius keeps referring not only to the "inaccessible light,"[9] but to the "dazzling obscurity of the secret Silence outshining all brilliance with the intensity of its darkness."[10] The mysteries of God are simple, absolute, and unchangeable, but they cannot be known, precisely because they are simple, absolute, and unchangeable, and we are not. Although God cannot be known, His place can be, and that is darkness, "the darkness of unknowing."[11] "He made darkness his secret place, and thick clouds cover him" (Psalm 18).

God is present in this darkness of unknowing, although still incomprehensible. He can be experienced, but not comprehended. Indeed, we must admit that this is true also of our experience of each other. No one can fully know himself or anyone else. Human personality is mysterious, however luminous. "Man is a great deep" (Augustine). Why should man then expect to find God any less mysterious?

Love Insatiable

For Dionysius the guiding image is darkness, for Gregory of Nyssa it is the cloud. Both are taken from the Old Testament, Dionysius being exegetically dependent on the Psalms, Gregory on Exodus 24. Probably the many other, and later, refer-

[8] Dionysius, *On the Divine Names*, p. 193.

[9] Dionysius, from a letter to Dorothy the Deacon, quoted by Evelyn Underhill in *Mysticism* (New York: Meridian Books, 1957), p. 347.

[10] Dionysius, *ibid.*, p. 191.

[11] *Ibid.*, p. 194.

ences to the cloud were themselves inspired by Exodus. "The Lord has said he would dwell in thick darkness" (II Chronicles 6:1), "clouds and darkness are round about Him" (Psalm 96:2).

> Then Moses went up on the mountain, and the cloud covered the mountain. The glory of the Lord settled on Mount Sinai, and the cloud covered it six days; and on the seventh day, he called to Moses out of the midst of the cloud. Now the appearance of the glory of the Lord was like devouring fire on the top of the mountain in the sight of the people of Israel. And Moses entered the cloud, and went up the mountain. And Moses was on the mountain forty days and forty nights.[12]

In his allegorical treatment of this passage Gregory reveals the major difference between him and Dionysius. The latter is concerned primarily with the effect of God on the mind of man. Man wants to see God, and he cannot: God dwells in darkness. Man wants to speak to God, and he can find nothing satisfactory to say; God is only silently present. Gregory too would know God, and his experience was similar to Dionysius', but for one thing. Gregory never forgot his desire for God, and he came to believe that insatiable desire is in itself the only reliable experience of God.

Gregory agrees with Dionysius that the divine nature is invisible, and he agrees that when man fully realizes this he has experienced a "vision" of God. "The true vision and the true knowledge of what we seek consists primarily in not seeing, in an awareness that our goal transcends all knowledge and is everywhere cut off from us by the darkness of incomprehensibility."[13] But this is indeed negative knowledge, and

[12] Exodus 24:15–18.

[13] *From Glory to Glory*, Texts from Gregory of Nyssa's Mystical Writings, selected by Jean Danielou, trans. Herbert Musurillo (New York: Charles Scribner's Sons, 1961), p. 29.

Gregory believed that something else was possible. If man were satisfied with this negative knowledge, he could not claim to have had a vision of God. But "the true vision of God consists rather in this, that the soul that looks up to God never ceases to desire Him. . . . The man who thinks that God can be known does not really have life."[14] The cloud of darkness is like a cloak which covers and protects. Within it much goes on between man and God. Man continues to desire God, meeting Him in love rather than knowledge. And because he continually desires, he is never satisfied; there is always more of God to meet. "This is the real meaning of seeing God: never to have this desire satisfied."[15] Or as Unamuno said, "The soul longs for a never-ending longing, for an eternal hope which is eternally renewed but never wholly fulfilled."[16]

If Gregory was right, then we should not be discouraged. What we should be satisfied with is not knowledge but unsatisfied desire. Only where desire for God is fading or seems to have vanished is there any reason to suspect that "God is dead." But if "each stage that we reach always reveals something heavy weighing on the soul,"[17] then theological thought has reached a higher stage of development than ever before. This is what must now be discussed, not whether God can be known. When Gregory meditated on the Song of Songs, he was attracted to the line from Chapter 5, "I sought Him but I could not find Him." He would have been interested in Lady Julian of Norwich's gloss on this, "I saw Him, and I sought Him; and I had Him, I wanted Him."[18] Man seeks God and does not find what he thinks he is looking for, but he finds God nonetheless.

[14] *Ibid.*, p. 56.
[15] *Ibid.*
[16] *The Tragic Sense of Life*, trans. J. E. Crawford Flitch (New York: Dover Publications, 1954), p. 256.
[17] Gregory of Nyssa, *From Glory to Glory*, p. 60.
[18] *Revelations of Divine Love* (London: Methuen 1952), p. 22.

He is perpetually beginning, making his future, torn by the ambiguity of expectation and heaviness of soul. As long as desire is ever-increasing, "union is endless."[19] "The true satisfaction of her desire consists in constantly going on in her quest and never ceasing in her ascent, seeing that every fulfillment of her desire continually generates a further desire for the Transcendent."[20]

The Cloud of Unknowing

The English mystical tradition of the fourteenth century knew Dionysius rather than Gregory, and yet it emphasized love in the darkness rather than ignorance and deprivation. The author of *The Cloud* reflected the influence of Dionysius when he wrote, "When I say darkness, I mean a lack of knowing . . . a cloud of unknowing which is betwixt thee and thy God."[21] The image stands for the ignorance of man and the incomprehensibility of God. The influence of this work is more humane than that of Dionysius' *The Mystical Theology*, for not only does its author say categorically that "God may well be loved, but not thought,"[22] that "love may reach to God in this life, but not knowing,"[23] he offers his readers especially wise counsel, as a master of the spiritual life should: "With a devout and a pleasing stirring of love . . . try to pierce that darkness above thee. And smite upon that thick cloud of unknowing with a sharp dart of longing love."[24] Life with God

[19] Gregory of Nyssa, quoted by Vladimir Lossky, *The Mystical Theology of the Eastern Church* (London: James Clarke, 1957), p. 35.

[20] Gregory of Nyssa, *From Glory to Glory*, p. 45.

[21] *The Cloud of Unknowing*, ed. Justin McCann (London: Burns Oates, 1960), pp. 12–13.

[22] *Ibid.*, p. 14.

[23] *Ibid.*, p. 19.

[24] *Ibid.*, p. 14.

is not, as with Meister Eckhart, "a desert of godhead where no one is at home," but a passion of heart with heart, man pressing forward, God responding.

Lady Julian of Norwich's *Revelations of Divine Love* should be read as a sequel to *The Cloud*. She too was confident of God's response to longing. God Himself languishes in love (compare the anonymous poem, "Quia amore langueo"). "The spiritual thirst of Christ, the love-longing that lasteth, and ever shall, till we see that sight on Doomsday,"[25] is more than a response to man's longing; it is the cause of it, "the ground of thy beseeching."[26] For "God is nearer to us than our own soul: He is the ground in whom our Soul standeth."[27] God wants us to want Him. He makes us want Him. He is within and with us in all our good resolutions and acts. He is felt most purely when we long for His love.

To Lady Julian God reveals himself as love. She understood everything about God in terms of this word. "Love was His meaning. Who shewed it thee? Love. What shewed He thee? Love. Wherefore shewed it He? For love."[28] No wonder that with this meaning a man's life can be judged happy. God had told her, "I may make all thing well, I can make all thing well, I will make all thing well, and I shall make all thing well; and thou shalt see thyself that all manner of thing shall be well."[29] The closer the soul gets to God, the more intimate, but the darker the analytical mind. The happier also the heart that loves and does not fear the transition from the busy intellect and senses to the strong but simple acts of the will, desiring, longing, resting in love.

[25] Lady Julian of Norwich, *Revelations of Divine Love*, p. 63.
[26] *Ibid.*, p. 84.
[27] *Ibid.*, p. 135.
[28] *Ibid.*, p. 202.
[29] *Ibid.*, p. 62.

Dark Contemplation—Dark Love

With St. John of the Cross the ambivalence of the dark
night of the soul was spelled out. For him the darkness was
deeper and, more typical of Western than Eastern spirituality,
admittedly unpleasant. For him also the darkness could be
joyously happy. For the first time, with St. John, the psychological and spiritual structures of the night were understood
and carefully described. "Night" was his favorite image, as
was "darkness" for Dionysius, "cloud" for Gregory and the
author of *The Cloud of Unknowing*. "Night" was Walter Hilton's image too. It is doubtful that St. John had even heard of
Hilton, but he would have warmly approved Hilton's description of "the good dark": "This is a night pregnant with good,
a glowing darkness, for it shuts out the false love of this world
and ushers in the dawn of the true day. Indeed, the darker this
night, the nearer the true day of the love of Jesus."[30] This is
what St. John was to call the "dark love,"[31] "this fire and thirst
of love,"[32] "the burning of love."[33] For him the way of contemplation is the way of loving, "a pure and dark contemplation,"[34] "a dark and secret contemplation."[35] When St. John
affirms that "faith is a dark night,"[36] we see no contradiction
of terms, but rather are meant to understand that faith is an
act inconceivable without love. The mystical tradition is the
strongest theoretical correction to a philosophical theology

[30] *The Ladder of Perfection* (Baltimore, Md.: Penguin Books, 1957), pp.
165–66.
[31] *The Collected Works of St. John of the Cross*, trans. Kieran Kavanaugh
and Otilie Rodriguez (New York: Doubleday 1964), p. 367.
[32] *Ibid.*, p. 358.
[33] *Ibid.*
[34] *Ibid.*, p. 333.
[35] *Ibid.*, pp. 318–19.
[36] *Ibid.*, p. 111.

that has forgotten the needs and dynamism of souls. Mystical theology always upholds the primacy of love, accepting the intrinsic limitations of love and insisting on unlimited longing. Once this is understood some of the obstacles and dilemmas facing religious intellectualism subside, and spirituality can be restored to its pre-eminent place.

Whoever now uses the expression "dark night of the soul" borrows from St. John of the Cross, who in a poem and in a commentary by that name imagined and explained a stage of spiritual development long known to mystics. Few are the men and women practiced in prayer even today who do not know this stage. Who of them can honestly say that he has never gone through a period of dryness, with the satisfactions of prayer left behind? St. John called this "the night of the senses," when it is normal for believers to become weary and to find prayer boring, even a drudgery, just as it is normal at other times for the same person to find peace and joy in prayer, whether private or liturgical. Perhaps it is a good thing to do without pleasure in prayer occasionally, so that one can be sure he is not praying for his own sake, but for the sake of God. "Dryness is best,"[37] at least part of the time, and is one aspect of the negative way to God.

Disappointing as the night of the senses is, it is not as discouraging, or as depressing as the dark night of the spirit. "The first purgation or night is bitter and terrible to the senses. But nothing can be compared to the second, for it is horrible and frightful to the spirit."[38] The night of the senses, with its "aridities and voids,"[39] cannot be compared with the

[37] *Spiritual Letters of Dom John Chapman* (London: Sheed and Ward, 1959), p. 99.
[38] St. John of the Cross, *Collected Works*, pp. 311–12.
[39] *Ibid.*, p. 323.

93

almost total depression of the spirit in the true dark night. Then the believer feels that God has abandoned him, and that his friends too have lost interest in him. The night of the spirit is, therefore, a night of complete solitude. Whereas in the night of the senses, a man loses interest in all that has been most important to him before, in the night of the spirit he feels that no one else has any interest in him. The analogy between the two nights and the ordinary psychological experiences of boredom and depression is obvious. The difference, perhaps only on the surface, is that the two nights involve man's conscious, as well as subconscious, relationship to God, and therefore contain a degree of explanation that may be lacking in everyday boredom and nonreligious depressive states.

Perhaps all depressive states are basically religious, in the sense that they are consequences of a person's sense of metaphysical void. If this is true, then it would be proper to think of one kind of depression as a consequence of a person's despair of finding God (or meaning, or love), and of another kind of depression as a consequence of despair of losing God. The feeling of a yawning void is common to both. There is a third kind of despair for those who have already despaired. This is the kind that Gerard Manley Hopkins was referring to in the following line from his journal: "I began to enter on that course of loathing and hopelessness which I have so often felt before."[40] His "terrible sonnets" are even more impressive than St. John of the Cross' discursive references (St. John's poems do not tell of the terrors of night at all):

> That night, that year
> Of now done darkness I wretch lay wrestling with (my God!)
> my God. (No. 41)

[40] *Sermons and Devotional Writings,* ed. Christopher Devlin (London: Oxford University Press, 1959), Retreat Notes in Ireland, January 1, 1888.

94

O the mind, mind has mountains; cliffs of fall
Frightful, sheer, no-man-fathomed. (No. 42)

I wake and fell the fell of dark, not day.
What hours, O what black hours we have spent
This night! What sights you, heart, saw; ways you went!
(No. 44)

If we are tempted to depreciate melancholy by saying that
some people are by nature melancholic, and even that some of
the most gifted human beings—Kierkegaard, Hopkins,
Woolf—were cursed with a melancholic disposition, we should
be reminded that they also had extraordinary periods of joy.
The last words of Hopkins were: "I am so happy. I am so
happy."[41] And there is the similar case of "The Little Flower,"
St. Teresa of Lisieux, whose happy death was preceded by
periods of great heaviness of soul, in which her faith became
all but obscured. "I get tired of the darkness all around me
. . . the country of darkness."[42] She wrote of the darkness
hiding God as a wall, and her own efforts in prayer as merely
efforts to believe despite her incredulity.

The truth about the dark night of the spirit is neither that it
is depressing nor that it is not lasting, but rather that it
represents a transition from illumination to subconscious
union of man and God. There are two movements that take
place at one time, on different levels, and are bound together
by a common intention, but because the old unity of spirit has
been suspended, the new experience, the hidden unity with
God, is not recognized and the soul suffers. This binding of
conscious and unconscious intentions is what later writers

41 *Poems and Prose of Gerard Manley Hopkins*, p. xxxi.
42 *Autobiography of a Saint*, trans. Ronald Knox (London: Fontana Books,
1960), p. 201.

called a "ligature."[43] While the soul wants to know and love God, the will is on the one hand firmly attached to God, but the mind and heart that have brought this to pass are left dangling, no longer needed. Unfortunately, the mind and heart have not yet understood this, and they go on trying to accomplish what has actually already been accomplished. One result is that both mind and heart can still be diverted by the loveliness of the world, and spirit has to keep them under control at the very time that it is, on a deeper level, settling down with God. Understood superficially, this means that one cannot put one's mind on two things at once, and, all the more difficult, when two levels—mind and spirit—are clashing.

The beginner at prayer knows nothing of the dark night of the spirit. His problem can be summed up in two words, laziness and distractions. Only the proficient know the dark night, those whose habit of longing for God is so firm that it no longer requires specific exercises of recollection, self-examination, and meditation, and does not even need to be encouraged by ecstasy, the first really intense experience of divine illumination. The dark night marks the entrance into union with God, so close and so quiet that compared to ecstasy or meditation—two quite different states—it often goes unnoticed. Whatever else union may mean, it is an "inflowing of God" responding smoothly and gently to the unceasing desire of man. This is what mystical theology calls "infused contemplation," and it is the ultimate stage in the progress of the soul toward full communion with God. It is to be sharply distinguished from the "touching" by knowledge of Plato and Plotinus, such an experience as is described by St. Augustine in his *Confessions:* "And then, in the flash of a trembling glance, my mind

---

[43] Chapman, *Spiritual Letters*, p. 61.

arrived at That Which Is. Now indeed I saw your invisible things understood by the things which are made, but I had not the power to keep my eye steadily fixed."[44] For the Platonic tradition, unlike the Christian mystical tradition, God is not essentially incomprehensible. What this means is that the God of Christians is a "god above gods," above the god of Plato and Plotinus, and can be met fully only in love. The test for the authenticity of the dark night of the soul is discovering whether in the heart of darkness the soul wants, like St. Teresa of Lisieux, to go on loving. "The only thing I want badly now is to go on loving till I die of love."[45] That is about as good a description of the significance of the dark night as can be found. For, as St. John has pointed out, the only way one can tell whether the feeling of void symbolizes loss of faith or increase of faith is to notice whether the soul abandons itself to the cares and seductions of the world.

The dark night comes without warning, and is endured for some time before it is understood.

> I entered into unknowing
> And there I remained unknowing,
> Transcending all knowledge.[46]

The first use of the word "unknowing" is ambivalent, a noun and also an adjective. Unknowing is a place, as darkness is said to be the place where God dwells. It will turn out to be something better than knowing, a loving. The soul enters it without knowing what is happening, and may remain there without awareness for a time. This is why a dark night seems darker and more depressing on successive occasions, not be-

---

[44] *Confessions*, Book VII, Chapter 18, p. 154.

[45] *Autobiography of a Saint*, p. 202.

[46] "Stanzas concerning an ecstasy experienced in high contemplation," *Collected Works of St. John of the Cross*, p. 718.

cause one has lost what one had before, but because it is so hard to keep on believing that one has not lost love at all, especially when the mind has gone on, as it must, about the many duties and cares of the day.

No one has stressed so clearly the secretive aspect of the dark night as St. John (compare Dionysius' "secret silence," "secret place"):

> Where have you hidden,
> Beloved, and left me moaning?
> You fled like the stag
> After wounding me.
> I went out calling You, and You were gone.[47]

In addition to distinguishing between knowledge and a state that is other, higher, more valuable, than knowledge, and in addition to assuring that God is hidden but not lost, St. John rejoices that the dark night is a happy night because in it the soul achieves the only perfection possible to man. Quietly, hardly knowing what it is about, but "wounded" by the heat of God's love, and with "no other light to guide than the one that burned in my heart,"[48] the soul is borne along in the stream of mutual love:

> For I know well the spring that flows and runs,
> Although it is night.
> That eternal spring is hidden,
> For I know well where it has its rise,
> Although it is night.[49]

This is the night (compare the Easter hymn "Exultet") "when heaven is wedded to earth, and God to man." This is the night

[47] "The Spiritual Canticle," *ibid.*, p. 712.
[48] "The Dark Night," *ibid.*, p. 711.
[49] "Song of the Soul that Rejoices in Knowing God through faith," *ibid.*, p. 723.

which began as man entered the cloud of unknowing, into the secret silence, wounded, lost, bewildered, and yet secure and finally happy in the arms of God. This is the night of sacrifice of earth for the love of heaven; this is the night when the sacrifice will be accepted so that earth may be redeemed and sanctified.

IV
The Meaning of
Darkness

6

The Neutrality of the Night

Light, light, more light! they tell us that the dying Goethe cried. No, warmth, warmth, more warmth! for we die of cold, and not darkness. It is not the night kills, but the frost.— Unamuno

Living in the Present

About one thing Pascal was wrong. Man does live in the present, whenever he is in darkness. The "fears and terrors of the night" may be unreal imaginings, but they are no less really felt in the present, and therefore they give their character to the present. We may grieve over the past and dread the future, but the grief and the dread are felt now, not then or later. In our feelings we live in the present and in no other time. We do cross bridges before we come to them, and we also fall off into the water. The fact that there really are no bridges and no water makes little difference. Whenever we act as if the past were present and the future already here, we are spending our time and our lives in the only time that does exist.

For many persons life has much more of darkness than of light. It is useless to try to persuade them that if the balance were the other way, they would be even worse off, mad or dead. The mind has a way of helping us endure darkness by temporarily bringing candles into the room. We are not altogether fooled by this; we cannot forget that the candle will burn down and the blackness close in again. We need a dif-

103

ferent metaphor. For some others it is as if they lived in a dark room which had become for them a prison from which they long to escape. They really believe escape is possible. Sometimes they even know how, sometimes they just about believe it is possible, but then admit that they have not quite found the way. Outside their prison there is another world, of light. They would not mind living most of the time in this dark room if they could be paroled occasionally into the light.

Darkness means many things to the same person. It can mean ignorance and isolation on the one hand, estrangement from meaning and direction, and, on the other hand, loneliness. It can also mean a refuge and center for exploration of meaning and intimacy. Under the cover of darkness man can experience opposites. In both cases a person is cut off almost completely from the world he has taken for granted, for ill or for good. One of the signs that he is cut off is that life measurably slows down and he experiences, often for the first time, the present. The degree of concentration hidden under cover of darkness is the measure of the awareness of the present as a mode of apprehension. It is also one of the conditions of experiencing reality as either very absent or very present. Darkness is an image of absence and an image of presence, in short the most radical imaging of reality possible.

Man is put on trial most severely in experiences of absence and isolation, in tragic suffering, and in depressions and breakdowns as well. When he reflects on the limits of human existence, the rational conclusions he reaches usually confirm his more passive apprehensions. It is not necessary to be part of a tragedy to conclude that God is far away. Nor is it necessary to suffer a nervous breakdown to conclude that control and sanity rest on flimsy foundations. All this one's intellect can admit, if it wishes to. It does not always wish to.

The complacency of normally busy and nonreflective persons is as resistant as the arrogance of some intellectuals who are so impressed by their own talents that they really believe at times in salvation by theory. Even natural catastrophe or personal failure do not necessarily have the power to make them see the real problems of life which the social sciences do not even consider. One would like to say to them, "You haven't the faintest idea what concerns me. You don't know what it is like to suffer, the way the world looks to the sufferer. Come into the darkness with me, and then you will know."

The philosopher on his lecture platform, the preacher in his pulpit, look and sound confident. But so does a clown in the ring. Remove a man from the environment where he has a role to play, and he will be like anyone else without his clothes, "poor bare forked animal."[1] Let him feel the storm, the isolating darkness of the night. Who is there to hear his lectures or his sermons, who besides himself will be comforted by them? True, we are, most of us, comforted by the society and approval of others. Were it otherwise, universal education, the thousands of pastoral comforters and sages, would by this time have relieved the desolation of the despondent. The duller sort could be cured by encapsulated reason and instant theology, while the lively intellects rejoice in games and syllogisms. In fact, they already do, and that is a great pity, for the test of humanity is not whether one can live without darkness but whether one can live without illusion.

Man does not live by reason—more often he just lives by bread. He lives by "hints and guesses,"[2] and above all by doing. The only life that has totally failed is the life that is

[1] Shakespeare, *King Lear*, Act III, scene iv, line 102.
[2] T. S. Eliot, "The Dry Salvages," V, line 29, *The Complete Poems and Plays* (New York: Harcourt, Brace, 1952), p. 136.

paralyzed. Man is meant to move and act, and he finds meaning in what he does and in what is done to and with him. Both Pascal and Newman, patrons of the wisdom of the heart, knew this. The former said, "The metaphysical proofs of God are so remote from the reasoning of men, and so complicated, that they make little impression."[3] And the latter, "I am far from denying the real force of the arguments in proof of a God, but these do not warm me or enlighten me; they do not take away the winter of my desolation, or make the buds unfold and the leaves grow within me, and my moral being rejoice."[4] At best they are pointers toward a country of truth that has to be explored on foot over a lifetime.

Mystery and Martyrdom

Is there ultimate meaning, so universal that it can be expressed for all men and chosen by all men? Is there cosmic support for lonely man? Is there God and all the rest, or just all the rest? Make up your mind, says Pascal, while you can. This is not a game to entertain those whose hearts are easy, but a game by which one can win or lose all, courage or collapse. "According to reason you can do neither the one thing nor the other; according to reason you can defend neither of the propositions,"[5] that God is or is not. Today, who does not say "yes" to that? But we must choose, we cannot stand neutral, except in words. You cannot stay neutral, even though the evidence is neutral. Either you believe or you do not, either you care or you do not, regardless of what you pretend. Pascal, and some others since, was exasperated by the indifference of those who do not care one way or another and kill time

[3] *Pensées,* par. 542.
[4] *Apologia pro Vita Sua,* pp. 217–18.
[5] *Pensées,* par. 233.

avoiding the dark. It is playing with words, I think, to say as Tillich does, that even they have a God, an "ultimate concern." And had Pascal forgotten the legion of nominal believers whose pretensions are as hollow as the unfevered agnosticism of the confessed skeptics? To all these we now add a new human type, men who, after some great test of faith, admit that all along their believing was only a valiant effort to believe, a "beautiful construct."[6] The fact that their effort was taken for sincere belief removes nothing from the poignancy of their disillusionment; it witnesses all the more vividly to the ambiguity of the human spirit. To those who want to keep trying, Pascal's advice is still sound: "At least learn your inability to believe . . . follow the way by which they began: by acting as if they believed. What have you to lose? What harm will befall you in taking this side? You will be faithful, honest, humble, grateful, generous, a sincere friend, truthful."[7]

What have you to lose? Only your intellectual integrity, of course. And will that really be offset by some gain to your character? This is like saying that the value of a belief is to be attested by its effect on character and behavior. Perhaps it is. In Pascal's case this may have been true, and yet one might wonder whether moral effects have any necessary relation to the theological hypothesis. Quite apart from the overwhelming evidence that many Christians are not men of good character at all, is not the evidence equally overwhelming that many men of good character are by no means usually Christian?

Cannot man believe in a way of life without believing im-

[6] Charles Davis, as quoted in *The National Catholic Reporter*, January 4, 1967; "So much of what I have written about the life of the Church . . . is a beautiful construct. It hangs together beautifully, theoretically. But it doesn't connect with concrete human experience."

[7] *Pensées*, par. 233.

plicitly or explicitly in some metaphysical scheme of things? This is a difficult (impossible?) question to answer, because it is hard to be certain that such a belief is altogether lacking in those who feel sure they have no faith and yet who live responsibly, confidently, joyously, and with full awareness of the powers of darkness. Faith is not always explicit enough to be identified, particularly by those who are intelligent enough to rebel against literal, grotesque, or sentimental expressions of religion. They sometimes believe more than they know. We would be careless to assume too readily that this distinction between implicit and explicit faith can relieve us from serious doubts about the need for absolutely defensible religion.

Maybe it would be prudent to fall back on the prepared position of classical religion that reality is essentially mysterious, that God is hidden because He is incomprehensible, or to remember Pascal's practical counsel: act, do, make. Let your dreams and wagers, your theories and beliefs, dress your actions, limning the flesh with the spiritual longing borne by concepts and images. "We speak the wisdom of God in a mystery, even the hidden mystery."[8] For Pascal and Paul, as for all Christians, this mystery was revealed in the life of Christ, and in the society inspired by faith in that life, "rooted and grounded in love."[9] "We know God only by Jesus Christ. Without this mediator all communion with God is taken away; through Jesus Christ we know God."[10] The mystery of Jesus, as retold by Pascal in the fragment of that name, is the same mystery that has given people strength to endure martyrdom. What jaded modern Christian can be sure that when put to the test he too will not affirm as never before his longing for this

[8] St. Paul, I Corinthians 2:7.
[9] St. Paul, Ephesians 3:17.
[10] *Pensées*, par. 546.

"mystery of love"?[11] Who of us can tell now what he would be faithful to? Pascal came as near to catching the secret companionship in the martyr's choice in his line "Jesus will be in agony even to the end of the world. You must not sleep during that time."[12] The martyrs are those who refuse to sleep. Their secret, in turn, is revealed at last as a love which some of them did not know they had, for they had it rather than felt it. "Thou wouldst not seek Me, if thou didst not possess Me."[13]

We have come across this manner of reasoning in St. Augustine and St. Anselm. Let us believe so that we may understand. Indeed, we do believe because we have already understood. If we are right in believing, i.e. if there is a God to believe in, this dialectic can help to explain the paradox of wanting to believe and not being able to, believing and discovering that the unexpected new is strangely familiar. But if there is no God, then the fact of seeking God does not prove His existence. It all depends on what reality turns out to be. Can one ever know that for sure? The evidence may well be neutral.

If, unfamiliar with church-goers, one should be suddenly transplanted among them on a Sunday morning, he might not guess at first how neutral the evidence really is. It all depends on the point of view, whether one is impressed by apparent reverence and sincerity or whether he finds the sights and sounds of group conversations with Someone who is not there simply comical. At the bottom of a calendar widely used by clergyman is a line taken from a sermon of Phillips Brooks, "If you are really looking to God for help, He is sending you help although you do not know it." Let us imagine a conversation inspired by this maxim.

[11] Favorite phrase of Charles Williams.
[12] *Pensées*, par. 552.
[13] *Ibid.*

"Very fine, but what is your evidence, if I do not know it?"

"He is the silent, the hidden helper."

"But suppose I am not being helped?"

"Then either you are resisting help or you are actually getting help even though you do not know it."

"Well, what good is it if I don't know it?"

"Very good indeed, for either the help will have delayed effects, or effects other than what you are looking for. May I remind you of the collect for the sixth Sunday after Trinity, which says that God has 'prepared for those who love him such good things as pass man's understanding . . . promises which exceed all that we can desire.' God not only helps in mysterious ways, He helps according to His understanding of our needs. And we do not always know what we need."

"Granted, but what about the needs I do know about and that nobody is doing anything about?"

"Yes, there are such needs, I admit, but God may think it best for you not to have these taken care of, at least not for a while. His time is not ours. And besides, we can sometimes learn from being abandoned. Or I should say, feeling abandoned, since I do not believe God ever really abandons us."

"Bully for you. All I have learned is either that God does not give a damn or that there is no God."

"No, you are wrong. God wants to give you time to toughen your moral fiber."

"I'm toughening it, against Him."

"And He has His own reasons and His own rewards. In the words of the collect for the twelfth Sunday after Trinity, He will 'give more than either we desire or deserve . . . those good things which we are not worthy to ask.' "

"I can believe that, and that is why I don't want anything to do with Him. By the way, do we have to go on talking of this nonexistent being as if He existed?"

"Certainly not, we know nowadays that it is inaccurate to speak of God's existence. His reality is too different from ours to make use of words we use about ourselves, except 'presence' perhaps."

"Come now, are there any words left that we do not use about ourselves? We use 'presence' all the time. And in any case, this is what we have been talking about. I have been asking you to tell me in what way He is present that I have missed, and you have not."

"Have you read . . . ?"

Longing

Freud and Tillich looked at the same facts and interpreted them differently. Tillich's "answering theology," his "method of correlation," tries to show how neatly Christian symbolism fits human need. Freud thought that this very neatness suggested illusion, wishful thinking. The evidence for the transcendent is, to some extent, neutral. And yet finitude and sin, to use the two existential categories that Tillich makes so much of, have not become innocuous to man come of age. How can man outgrow the consequences of his mortality or his fallibility? Longing experienced in darkness, tragic, melancholic, metaphysical, religious covers so much more than what is implied by the word "question." It may be too much to speak of tragic exaltation or the good dark, when all one has a right to speak of is the opposite, but it is more perilous to ignore the crying of the spirit of man as he waits for grace. One thing we can be sure of: such a spirit will find no consolation in the theological message that God is "absolute future," or "process." A cry wants a human response, and this is why at least some of those people praying away in churches, however comical they may look to the skeptic in us, are in some sense in the right.

And if there is no response? That is a difficult supposition to live with. Perhaps an unconscious motive behind much theological speculation is the wish to avoid thinking this at a level where it will hurt. When one comes to think of it, it is amazing that so many pages can be written about God and so few deal with this most heart-sundering problem. It is difficult not to suspect that God-games in the classroom are much like war-games in the living room, the principal difference being that the former require a degree in theology. "But suppose that what you are up against is a surgeon whose intentions are wholly good. The kinder and more conscientious he is, the more inexorably he will go on cutting."[14] So C. S. Lewis in his private anguish, still believing and still trying to understand how and why one he had trusted could, apparently, turn away from one he had loved. His analogy from the workaday world sprang from a terrible hurt: he could think the analogy, but he could not inject trust back into it.

How far apart is the perspective of one who suffers from one who, at the moment, does not. Listen to one of our (otherwise) most perceptive theologians, Karl Rahner: "If your love of me were so manifest that I could ask no more anxious questions about it, if You had made absolutely clear the most important thing about me, namely, that I am someone loved by You, how then could I prove the daring courage and fidelity of my love? How could I even have such love? Your love has hidden itself in silence, so that my love can reveal itself in faith. You have left me, so that I can discover You."[15] Rahner's piety is obvious, but it reveals his willingness to settle for a very small deity who plays callous games with humans. What is there to love in such a god? He is like a pretty girl who pretends she is not interested in her suitors in order to provoke them into

[14] *A Grief Observed*, p. 36.

[15] Karl Rahner, *Encounters with Silence* (Westminster, Md.: Newman Press, 1960), p. 56.

making fools of themselves. Why should God not make His love "so manifest" that we could ask no more questions about it? What is wrong with that? Why should God not make it absolutely clear that He loves us? Is this not what theologians usually claim God did when He sent His son to live and die for us? And is it true that man is more likely to love that which he does not see than that which he does see? Surely, all the evidence is to the contrary.

The following passage from Teilhard de Chardin might have been written to contest Rahner's argument, if Teilhard de Chardin had not been dead when Rahner wrote that passage. "Scholars explain that the Lord deliberately hides himself in order to test our love. One has to be hopelessly lost in intellectual games, or never to have encountered either in oneself or others the sufferings of doubt, not to see what is detestable in such an answer. O my God, your creatures stand before you, lost and in anguish, appealing for help. To have them rush at you, it would be enough to show them a single ray of your light, the fringe of your cloak—and you would not do this for them?"[16] The piety is as evident as Rahner's, but it is of a different order. Teilhard does not apologize for God's silence by praising it; he simply cries for help. He believes and he doubts, and he will not go beyond the evidence of his heart.

What is the evidence worth? Is longing the same as belief,

[16] Pierre Teilhard de Chardin, quoted in Christopher Mooney's *Teilhard de Chardin and the Mystery of Christ* (New York: Harper and Row, 1966), p. 144. Cf. "Either there is an escape from death—somewhere—for an individual's thought, for his self-consciousness, or else the world is a hideous mistake. And if it is, then there is no use in our going on. But, since the uselessness of going on is an idea intolerable to everyone, the alternative must be to believe. To awaken this belief shall be, now more than ever, my task. I swear it." Quoted by Mrs. Joan Gill in her letter to the editor of *The National Catholic Reporter*, June 8, 1966. But is this belief really the only alternative? Surely not, since many "go on" who do not believe.

wishing to believe as believing? Those who answer "yes" are in good company, a varied company, as varied as Tillich, Unamuno, and Dom John Chapman. "To believe is to wish to believe, and to believe in God is, before all and above all, to wish that there be a God."[17] "It is not necessary to want God and want nothing else. You have only to want to want God, and want to want nothing else. Few get beyond this really."[18] Dom John Chapman was a master of souls, and if anyone knew about this sort of thing, he did. His judgment makes Unamuno's heterodoxy begin to look respectable. Their conviction does, however, beg the question; it repeats and does not explain. Tillich's explanation may be a rephrasing in more technical language, but it does at least suggest a hidden dynamism that might be used as a working hypothesis.

Tillich was always curious about the power and persistence that make possible several states of mind that on the surface look quite different: despair, endurance, courage, and faith. What is the ultimate source of endurance? Where does the energy for crushing despair come from? How can one believe in God when there is no obvious evidence that there is God? The problems are similar. How can affirmations be made without reason and in the face of stony silence? Nothing in the life of the individual as individual or as human seems to explain. Tillich's answer is beautifully simple. If I do not have in me the answer, then someone else must be supplying it for me. "Faith is the state of being grasped by the power of being-itself."[19] "The acceptance of despair is in itself faith and on the boundary line of the courage to be. . . . As long as this

[17] Unamuno, *The Tragic Sense of Life*, p. 114.
[18] Chapman, *Spiritual Letters*, p. 46.
[19] *The Courage To Be*, p. 172. See also Leslie Dewart, *The Future of Belief*, pp. 175–78, for a "proof" of the reality of God.

despair is an act of life it is positive in its negativity."[20] This means that Tillich feels that whether one accepts despair and goes on with life, or more boldly affirms his faith, he may feel that he is being moved by God. And if someone chooses to die, he chooses not to be moved, and that too is an affirmation testifying to divine energy, although a limited affirmation. The fate of man lies ultimately, according to this analysis, in the degree to which the mind of man understands the power which is at his disposal. But here is where the mystery of human nature really appears, in this understanding and its elusive freedom. Perhaps Tillich has solved one question, by hypothesizing a God who moves man, only to lay bare a more haunting mystery, the freedom of man to understand the saving grace of this power. Why do we not always see it Tillich's way? Why sometimes, even so, do we still choose to ignore it? Finally, if man is free to accept or reject, why not also suppose that he has no power, no being except his own to move or be moved by, and that this alone is what his freedom works with?

Beyond Illusion

Twisted and elusive as the question of faith can be, it is not as agonizing as the question posed by death. St. Paul put it very simply, "If our hope in Christ has been for this life only, we are the most unfortunate of all people."[21] Indeed, this Pauline agony, however suppressed by contemporary theology, may well be the secret motive compelling mankind to persist in seeking God. It is their failure (or is it really disinterest?) to talk seriously about death that makes so much theology seem irrelevant. We should be grateful to Unamuno

[20] *The Courage To Be*, p. 175.
[21] I Corinthians 15:19.

for trying so hard to make us remember our mortality. He may not have been orthodox, and he certainly was not a technically expert theologian, but he understood the basic concerns of orthodox Christians and of ordinary doubters of the twentieth century as well. He spent his life longing not to die, and seeking and inventing reasons to believe that he would not. There has never been a more poignant witness to the agony of being alive, and knowing that we will not always be, than this great soul. Who knows whether he ever resolved the torment of his longing and his doubting?

His story "St. Emmanuel the Good, Martyr," so much more than the better known *The Tragic Sense of Life*, presents this tension between hope and skepticism. It is the story of a village priest in Spain, whose outward charity and joy are so dynamic that his people regard him as a saint, but whose inner skepticism is so profound that he pretends faith only out of love for his parishioners. "The truth is perhaps something so unbearable, so terrible, something so deadly, that simple people could not live with it. . . . The important thing is that they live sanely, in concord with each other—and with the truth, with my truth, they could not live at all. . . . There is no other life but this, no life more eternal . . . let them dream it eternal . . . let it be eternal for a few years."[22] This is now called "Christian atheism." What distinguished Unamuno from ourselves was that he could not reconcile himself to this.

In a tortured passage at the end of the story, the narrator, a friend of the dead Don Emmanuel, sums up—and we may be sure for Unamuno as well: "I am of the opinion that Don Emmanuel the Good, my Don Emmanuel, and my brother too,

[22] *Abel Sanchez and Other Stories*, trans. Anthony Kerrigan (Chicago: Gateway Edition, 1956), p. 238.

died believing that they did not believe, but that, without believing in their belief, they actually believed, with resignation in desolation. I believed then, and I believe now, that God, as part of I know not what sacred and inscrutable purpose—caused them to believe they were unbelievers. And I, do I believe? Do I really understand any of it? Do I really believe in any of it?"[23] Who can tell? Who can tell for sure whether longing is the same as believing? To say, as Tillich does with such assurance, that doubt is always present within active faith, does not answer the question either, it just begs it. If there is God, then there is faith; and if there is faith, why not admit doubt as part of its dynamic tension? But is there God, is there God to guarantee resurrection? And is this resurrection individual or collective, cosmic or personal? The Christian affirmation about man's future depends on the paradigmatic resurrection of one, Jesus Christ, and on the moral effects of that belief in subsequent history. Unfortunately, the biblical text itself can be questioned, doubted, explained this way or that, and we are left with the wish to believe it, with no sure confirmation of either the truth about history or the shape of things to come.

On so little so much has depended for so long. This can be understood best by those who suffer greatly, and especially by those who like C. S. Lewis are left desolate by the death of a loved one. His wife's death had, to use his image, slammed a door between him and God. His desolation was real, and yet after some days he began to feel "that the door is no longer shut and bolted."[24] His response was to "stop bothering." "And the remarkable thing is that since I stopped bothering

23 *Ibid.*, pp. 262–63.
24 *A Grief Observed*, p. 38.

117

about it, she seems to meet me everywhere."[25] Then the wisdom of the night began to be heard. "One moment last night . . . the idea that I or any mortal at any time may be utterly mistaken as to the situation he is really in. . . . How much of total reality can such an apparatus let through?" And finally he recorded "that impression which I can't describe except by saying that it's like the sound of a chuckle in the darkness. The sense that some shattering and disarming simplicity is the real answer."[26] Or, as he later summed up, "The best is perhaps what we understand least."[27] Lewis was theologically sophisticated enough to know by heart, even if he had not actually read, the entire stock of question-begging apologies for belief. He had reasoned his way into belief, and had been "surprised by joy."[28] He had been given love late in life, and lost it almost as soon as he found it. He was not one to pretend or to live with illusions without telling himself what he was doing. His testimony, therefore, coming out of grief, is worth something, if only to underline the power and persistence of the will to live and to function sanely. It shows more than that. He calls our attention to two neglected truths about the human mind. However often we protest awareness of the mind's limitations, we seldom acknowledge a positive corollary of those limits. Not only is there a vast area blocked off to understanding at any time, it may well be that the most important truths, most useful to us if we knew them, are precisely the ones that we are fated to know least well, or not at all. In addition, there are truths, so central, so intimate that we would not be able to live at all, or live happily, without living by them. We take much

[25] *Ibid.*, p. 42.
[26] *Ibid.*, p. 56.
[27] *Ibid.*, p. 59.
[28] Title of his autobiography.

for granted that looks plain and ordinary, and in the end we find we have called hidden what has always been active and out in the open. For we are saved not by argument, analysis, or intentions, nor by memories and sentiments, but by things done.

7

The Wisdom of the Night

We shall struggle in the night, and we must do our best to endure this life without too much sadness. Let us stand by each other in the dark, and do justice as often as an opportunity is given.—Pierre Proudhon

The Act Is the Meaning

The biblical injunction to ask is not completed by "It will be answered," but by "It will be *given* to you." Man asks many questions that can be answered, and also some very important questions that cannot be answered by any words or explanations. Some of these cannot be answered at all, because they are nonsensical. And some can be satisfied only by deed, that is, by gift and act. In the darkness that covers both absence and presence, to ask a question about existence is an encouragement for acting out an answer. Presence can no more be explained, put into words, justified, than absence. Presence is the gift, or grace, that is missing in the experiences of loss and silence. When all things slow to a stop, the gift of life and hope has been almost used up. When life accelerates, the fullness of all that is being currently given is apprehended and enjoyed.

A child cries in the dark, and his mother runs to comfort him. As a man, the same child cries and love answers or turns away. The cry must arise, whether it speaks of presence or absence; and only when it is not allowed to run its course, must darkness fall and death take over. The meaning of the cry is in the darkness itself, the cry that embraces as it appre-

120

hends, or the cry that rises only to fall back in uncompleted agony. It is a waste of breath to ask for explanations of absence and loss and waste; only presence ever explains anything to our satisfaction. When we cry out in a vacuum—or what we fear is a vacuum—we are still crying for presence: "Come to me!" It is the same cry, starting off in the same way, with the same motive, the same direction. It is an act, and it can be understood fully only as a completed act, not a frustrated or abortive one. The meaning is always in some action: the meaning is always an act. To understand this perhaps one has to be fairly simple-minded, or unusually sophisticated (in order to cut through the entanglements of minds accustomed to verbal questions and verbal answers).

A biblically oriented mind ought to be able to understand this. "The Word was made flesh and dwelt among us."[1] This was the "answer" to the people who had walked in darkness. This act of God was to be their light, the light that would enlighten all that come into the world. God had acted before, and whenever He did, His act was like "light that darkness could not overpower."[2] The word is not as credible as the deed; and that is why the word had to become a deed. We are never so credible when we say "Listen to me," as we are when we say "Look at what I am doing." We can convince ourselves temporarily with arguments, but only presence in action unshakably convinces. Personal devotions to Jesus and his mother have throughout Christian history been more effective than the arguments of the theologians. We will not be saved by what we say, but by what we do and are. We are according to what we have received, and we cannot receive unless we are given.

[1] John 1:14 (Jerusalem Bible [New York: Doubleday, 1966]).
[2] *Ibid.*, 1:5.

121

The sign of the gift is the acceptance. The first lesson the learned and well-read must learn is stillness and acceptance. One must find out what he already is and go on from there. No one grows wise who has not learned to be ruthlessly honest with himself. But wisdom is very full and very hard to attain to. Much more than honesty is involved. Mankind has always, and now more than ever, confused knowledge and wisdom, the discrete explanations of discrete questions on the one hand, and the living unity of memory and desire, regret and anticipation, depression and hope, in short, nostalgia. Knowledge is always a means, not to wisdom only but to survival and enjoyment. Wisdom, on the other hand, should be thought of as a manner of life that has matured so that it can address anything that turns up, in freedom, stability, and selflessness. If we can learn to think of wisdom as the deeply experienced set of images, insights, and convictions that have become habitual, we may stop looking, in the manner of poor Job, for an explanation of darkness. The heart of darkness is not horror any more than it is joy. It is the place where God, ultimate presence, is felt as pressure for love. The greater the pressure, the more we fear darkness; the more our own longing is released—encouraged to be released—the more intimate the sense of presence, even in physical absence.

This explains why it is useful to think of God as a person, for persons, when unreservedly present, release us from the weight of fears and terrors. It explains too the interpenetration of longing with a sense of presence, and the indivisibility of longing and presence, of question and action. We are and have so much more than we usually realize: insight, affection, art, imagination, the past, freedom for some future, work to be done, people to take care of. All these, in proportions unique for every man, comprise the integrity of longing, the structure and the content of the movement in, around, and out of the levels of consciousness. The analytically clever man gets into a habit of breaking all this up into parts, and his own natural totality becomes fragmented and disturbed. He looks for a lost unity outside himself, and, of course, like St. Augustine, never finds it—at least until he begins to look at longing differently.

There is nothing more basic to personality than longing. It can go either way, so to speak, terribly broken into black darkness, or joyously united to luminous darkness. Which way it goes will depend on experience, on witnesses and examples, and on one's own understanding of its meaning. Just as there is a spectrum of darkness, from boredom right through to death, so there is a spectrum of nostalgia, from wishing right through to union. And just as the spirit of a man can fall rapidly from one level of unhappiness to another, so swiftly that the last stage includes all the rest, so nostalgia includes all the modes and pitches of presence, the intimations and the acts that make up the meaning and integrity of a person's life. It is proper to mention integrity, that fundamental unity of meaning that makes a unified moral resolution possible. The personal continuity that underlies a promise, consistency of purpose, and commitment across time, reflects an interior unity that is normally taken for granted. All my life leads up to this moment, whether the moment be contemplative or active. All the past, its reservations and its qualities, its poignant reachings out or its firmly held appreciations, all the past together with the habitual rhythm of waiting and moving, all the kaleidoscopic designs of mind and spirit, contribute to the formation of this moment, right now. As we talk to others, we reveal bit by bit to them the pattern of our lives, and they the same to

123

us. Only art can represent it adequately in its living integrity so that the essential uniqueness and mystery can be captured.

Few do or can tell the whole truth about themselves. Most do not know it. Only partial truths or conscious lies answer the importunate, the idle question. We need a transitory identity so badly, for this occasion or that, that we get into the habit of deluding ourselves as well. How often we play roles, not only in daydreams, but in our normal occupations as well, as parents, workers, players, lovers, makers. Not only do we pretend to be better, bigger, than we really are, we pretend to be wholly other than we are also. After a while integrity becomes self-fooling and pretense.

This is so true that it is possible to wake up one morning and realize we do not know who we are, what we believe in, what has been going on inside us all these years. "The night is far spent,"[3] without the day being at hand. The awakening is usually only temporarily demoralizing. But it may be a chance to see ourselves for the first time. Like good cinema writers and directors we must learn to contemplate the features that make up the wholes that we really are, and by placing some of these features side by side, to reveal the person behind our successive masks. Or it would be as if we had drawn from the Tarot-like pack of our fragmented personality the major trumps. Considering each in turn, arranging them in different orders, considering them also side by side in these orders, we might uncover their internal associations and depths. There, as all we have felt and known, all we have desired, and all we have become, as these all become present, the barriers between us and everything we experience fade and we merge with a swirling world of presences where longing is grounded in real satisfaction. Such contemplation is like a conversation in the

[3] St. Paul, Romans 13:12.

124

dark where only the truth is spoken and that truth is absolutely basic.

While this uncovering of the self may be called contemplation, its real nature is nostalgic. Even as contemplating takes place in stillness, it progresses by expanding out beyond its center until it touches and merges with all experience. This is an act of love, with or without bodies present, nostalgic only because it embraces past and future as well as present, and loving insofar as it combines desire and acceptance in one gesture. To those who ask what is to be done with unsatisfied longing, the answer is clear: rejoice, for this is the road to paradise. "We can't know whether love is a proof of the existence of God or whether love is God in person."[4] We are, as it were, created in His image, inexhaustible loving. Match Him, meet Him, in unsatisfied longing. Man wants a longer finality than death. He can have it if he accepts the lasting longing. But he must first agree to ignore the question as to whether there is "another life" that would give meaning to "this life." Not only because man cannot know about "another life," but because it is an irrelevant question for anyone who is busy loving in this life. So many irrelevant questions are products of a slowing-down of energies and interests, and disappear face to face in the intimacies of darkness.

One fair question is left. Is it enough to know that there is love in the world? Hope comes from knowing that there is love, all kinds of love. But suppose there is none for me? Nobody who keeps on trying to love remains unloved. But he must keep trying. He must be a witness to the unifying power of longing. The fragments lost in horrible darkness will be gathered into one, and some others leaving that darkness will

[4] Ingmar Bergman, *Une Trilogie*, p. 110.

be responsive witnesses to a new creation. Love may not create love, but it will find it sooner or later.

The World Outside

It was dark in the womb, but he could not remember that. "Out of darkness into marvellous light."[5] He would not know how marvellous for a long time, for he would be carrying much of that primeval darkness along with him.

The lighted area seemed very large when he was inside it. But when he drove beyond the suburbs into the country, beyond the street lights, past the sleeping farms, all the world seemed dark. He got out of the car and looked back at the glow over the city. What were they doing back there, shopping, looking, talking, laughing, keeping all those lights on so long? Were there that many cars chasing around with headlights blazing? It was too far away to be sure. It might be emptied of people; who can tell? Already in the quiet of the country he was forgetting what he had left behind.

Sometimes he tried a prayer or two before sleep, more often tried to begin where he had left off the night before, the sequel to the current serial of fantasy and recollection. It was a way of staving off disequilibrium at the fatigued end of the day. Like sacramental confession these final thoughts were meant to be distillations of failure and desire. The truer the confession, the more complete the absolution. What was the absolution other than a seal upon integrity?

In the morning he strove to extract from memory's vein the ore that could be refined for reconstruction of his integrity. Each piece of metal must be cut, shaped, polished until it

[5] I Peter 2:9.

126

shone with a special brightness. Each had to be fitted, notch and groove, into the sides of the others. He was determined to know how he was made, and the only way he could find out was to put himself together piece by piece.

The chrysanthemums in the warden's garden, the chapel organ, the flying surplices. As he strode over the meadowsweet to the sandy pool, the bells began their pealing from the village on the other side of the wood. At night when he went to the pillar box at the corner, the smell of many coal fires joined the other remembrances from a childhood across the sea.

From one hill the view over the blue islands, from another the green rolling crops. The hot summer sun in backyard or on beach.

Fog and rain, a steamer's whistle quavering in from the harbor, wind and spray, walks along the shore in gray weather. Then at last the geraniums, and sure resurgence of spring, like music by the fire.

In the fall burning leaves, in spring burning grass, and wind in the pines; in the fall crickets, in the spring small frogs, and summer days sown with cicadas. They met by chance or by appointment, with no exceptional greeting, no ultimate questions or rounder replies.

There is a night of disillusion and frustration, empty and failed, with desperate voids and impossible substitutes for loving. There is a night of treason, lies, bad dreams, disappearance, and death.

There is also a night—"This is the night"[6]—of expectation, of rebirth, of discovering and being discovered, of waiting in the dark and being met, by lamp post, in a clearing somewhere, for each a different place and a different time.

[6] Repeated in Easter Eve song, "Exultet."

Who but one who craves the sun can tell of the night? The upturned faces on the stone steps, soaking in the spring sun. Rite of warmth and love.

The World Within

The meaning is in the action, or is the action. "The Lord shall enlighten my darkness."[7] The chill faded when a child called his name, when he stood above the figures kneeling at the rail, when the dying man smiled. Why did he leave the gift at the foot of the statue? What did it mean when they sang hymns of liberation? What did it mean when a dead letter sent to her—alas, away—finally reached her and she replied? What did it mean to be held in someone's arms? What did it mean when a whole life's longing flowed unimpeded between high banks? There were no explanations, only satisfactions.

She saw him coming, and ran to him. It was only a dream, and they never met. Finally they did meet, and there was nothing to say. There ought to have been something, else it were better they stay with their dreams. There were such long silences that meant nothing at all. The cold got colder when they were together. They understood that they knew nothing of each other, nothing at all. Finally they ceased to think about it. Night was colder than they expected. How could they ever have believed protestations of agony? "So long as you are alive, I too will be alive. When you die, the world will be empty." They wanted to believe something in order to bring finality into an ephemeral universe. "You were sometimes darkness,"[8] and alas have remained.

The others had dreams too—the stuff of which reality is

[7] Psalm 18:29.
[8] St. Paul, Ephesians 5:8.

made—of meeting in a corridor of light. "You looked as if you belonged to me," he said; to which she replied, "But I do."

The final dark is but the vacuum left when man abandons dream and longing. The steel hidden in endurance on the far side of tragedy, the resolution that drags soul back from the vortex of demoralization, the fidelity to someone who is both present and absent, are remnants of the longing that still defines the integrity of man. There is no night so black or so cold that longing—to say nothing of union—cannot infuse with warmth and light. The first lesson of the night, therefore, is that it is always easier to move in it than to see in it. The last lesson is that under cover of darkness all the most important things happen: we are born, we learn, we create, we suffer, we make love. Darkness is our natural element, and we return to it for rest and union after the torments and deprivations of the day.

INDEX

Adams, H., 30, 31, 44
Amiel, 38
Anselm, 85, 109
Antonioni, 19, 22
Aristotle, 51, 53, 56
Auden, 7
Augustine, 20, 30, 31, 67, 73, 87, 96, 109, 123

Barth, 85
Beauvoir, de, 51
Beckett, 21
Bergman, 29, 71, 72, 74, 76, 77, 125
Bernanos, 20
Bonhoeffer, 64, 75
Brooks, P., 109

Camus, 8, 69, 70, 71, 72, 74
Chapman, 93, 96, 114
Chronicles, 88
Cloud of Unknowing, 84, 90, 91
Conrad, 11, 42
Cox, 86

Davis, 107
Dewart, 86, 114*n*
Dionysius, 84–88, 90, 92, 98
Dostoevsky, 19, 22, 23, 45*n*, 56, 77

Eckhart, 91
Eliot, 82, 105
Epicurus, 77
Exodus, 87, 88

Fitzgerald, 26, 34
Forster, 24

Fortunatus, 37
Freud, 111

Genesis, 3
Goldmann, 45, 74–75
Gregory of Nyssa, 84, 87–90, 92

Hemingway, 3, 48
Hilton, 92
Homer, 36
Hopkins, 34, 75, 94–95

Isaiah, 66

Jaspers, 50
Job, 44, 45, 122
Joyce, 10, 44, 53
Julian of Norwich, 89, 91
Jung, 44, 58

Kafka, 21, 40, 49
Kierkegaard, 4, 19, 20
Koestler, 33
Krieger, 55
Krutch, 46–47, 51

Latin Hymns, 34, 127
Lermontov, 23
Lewis, C. S., 78–80, 112, 117–18
Lukàcs, 49, 73, 75
Lynch, 43, 55

Marx, 48
Melville, 5
Miller, A., 49
Mitchell, B. G., 80–81
Montaigne, 66

131

This book was set in eleven-point Bodoni Book type. It was composed, printed, and bound by Kingsport Press, Inc., Kingsport, Tennessee. The paper is Warren's Olde Style, manufactured by S. D. Warren Company, Boston. The design is by Mary Thomas.

RL

EYIRR

HARPER